The Gift of Second

The Gift of Second

Healing from the Impact of Suicide

Brandy Lidbeck

Unless otherwise noted, scriptures taken from the Holy Bible, New International Version®, NIV®. Copyright © 1973, 1978, 1984, 2011 by Biblica, Inc.™ Used by permission of Zondervan. All rights reserved worldwide. www.zondervan.com The "NIV" and "New International Version" are trademarks registered in the United States Patent and Trademark Office by Biblica, Inc.™

Scripture quotations are taken from the Holy Bible, New Living Translation, copyright ©1996, 2004, 2007, 2013, 2015 by Tyndale House Foundation. Used by permission of Tyndale House Publishers, Inc., Carol Stream, Illinois 60188. All rights reserved.

R.T. Kendall, *Total Forgiveness* (Lake Mary, FL: Charisma House, 2002). Used by permission.

Some content taken from *Quiet Strength: A Memoir* by Tony Dungy. Copyright © 2007. Used by permission of Tyndale House Publishers, Inc. All rights reserved.

"Book One: Italy", from EAT PRAY LOVE: ONE WOMAN'S SEARCH FOR EVERYTHING ACROSS ITALY, INDIA AND INDONESIA by Elizabeth Gilbert, copyright © 2006 by Elizabeth Gilbert. Used by permission of Viking Books, an imprint of Penguin Publishing Group, a division of Penguin Random House LLC. "Any third party use of this material, outside of this publication, is prohibited. Interested parties must apply directly to Penguin Random House LLC for permission."

Excerpt(s) from ILLUMINATA: THOUGHTS, PRAYERS, RITES OF PASSAGE by Marianne Williamson, copyright © 1994 by Marianne Williamson. Used by permission of Random House, an imprint and division of Penguin Random House LLC. All rights reserved. "Any third party use of this material, outside of this publication, is prohibited. Interested parties must apply directly to Penguin Random House LLC for permission."

Excerpt(s) from TRAVELING MERCIES: SOME THOUGHTS ON FAITH by Anne Lamott,
copyright © 1999 by Anne Lamott. Used by permission of Pantheon Books, an imprint of the Knopf Doubleday Publishing Group, a division of Penguin Random House LLC. All rights reserved. "Any third party use of this material, outside of this publication, is prohibited. Interested parties must apply directly to Penguin Random House LLC for permission."

ISBN-9780998074702 (Gift Pub)
ISBN-0998074705
Library of Congress Control Number: 2016914713
Gift Pub, Grass Valley, CA

Cover Design by Bethany Beams. Cover Photo by Prixel Creative.

I dedicate this book to those who, like me, continue on the journey toward healing after the loss of a loved one to suicide. It is truly the club we never wanted to be in, but I am so relieved there are others who understand what this membership is like.

Table of Contents

A Letter from the Author

"Empathy is about finding echoes of another person in yourself."

—Mohsin Hamid

I AM INCREDIBLY heartbroken that you, too, know the devastation and grief a suicide brings. I am sorry you have experienced one of the darkest and most challenging losses of this world.

Too many times, as survivors, we feel alone and isolated and believe nobody could ever understand the depth of grief, shock, anger, guilt, sadness, shame, and loss that is unique to a suicide death. It wasn't until thirteen years after my mom's passing that I even met another person who had experienced a suicide, which only compounded my feelings of being alone. I have written this book with one goal in mind: to create a valuable resource covering a multitude of topics pertaining to suicide that would benefit all survivors, regardless of where they are in their journey.

I am writing this book from three different roles all wound together into what I hope is a treasured resource for you and your family as you walk this path.

First, I have experienced suicide two times. At ten years old I walked into my home to find my mom's body after she took her own life. My dear cousin also killed himself shortly after returning home from his military service in Iraq. Suicide has devastated our family.

Second, I am a licensed marriage and family therapist and have included clinical information pertaining to grief, trauma, forgiveness, and self-care. I spell out what is normal to experience after a suicide and when to seek professional help.

Finally, I am the creator of *The Gift of Second*, a website for those impacted by the suicide of a loved one (thegiftofsecond.com). *The Gift of Second* contains a myriad of video testimonies and blogs contributed by fellow survivors. After countless interviews and conversations with the courageous people willing to share their story with others, I began asking hundreds of fellow survivors for help in writing this book. I asked them what content they felt should be covered, which resources have been helpful, and what wisdom they would pass on to other survivors. Their responses were both heartbreaking and relatable on many levels. Their willingness to be open and vulnerable enabled me to compile priceless information pertaining to feelings, experiences, and wisdom that I will pass on to you in this book. Their responses were both informative and healing to my own heart. May it be the same for you.

In the following pages, I have covered a wide variety of subjects with both honesty and vulnerability as I attempt to normalize all that you are likely feeling in the wake of your loved one's suicide. Far too often we go through life alone, refusing to mention the suicide for fear of how others might react and what they may think, or fear of the emotions we may, ourselves, produce. It's a shame that any of us would ever suffer in silence. I want to open up the dialogue and allow for an honest conversation to occur.

Brené Brown once stated, "The two most powerful words when we're in struggle: me too."

Mostly, I want you to know you are not alone. We understand. Me too.

Sincerely,
Brandy

CHAPTER 1

The Path of Grief

"Grief is not a disorder, a disease or a sign of weakness. It is an emotional, physical and spiritual necessity, the price you pay for love. The only cure for grief is to grieve."

— DR. EARL GROLLMAN

AFTER A SUICIDE, the emotions we experience are unpredictable. We feel as if we will never be 'normal' again. We feel crazy! In the foreword for the book *A Grief Observed* by C.S. Lewis, Madeleine L'Engle writes, "The death of a beloved is an amputation." I agree. Most of us want a timeline for how long we can expect to feel this way, and many have expressed that death would be better than experiencing what a survivor does in the wake of a suicide. Unfortunately, there is no specific answer for how long grieving lasts. Dr. Earl A. Grollman, a certified Death Educator and Counselor explains, "Each person's grief journey is unique as a fingerprint or a snowflake." Although an equation of A+B= Grief Relief would be enthusiastically received, grief has no absolutes.

In 1969, after extensive research with dying individuals, Elisabeth Kübler-Ross, a Swiss-American psychiatrist, created the theory that people grieve in stages. She discovered that each person, near death, experienced a series of stages as the end of their life drew near: denial, anger, bargaining, depression, and acceptance. Widely used in the mental health profession and accepted in the general population as well, this concept has since been commonly adopted by the world to describe the stages an individual goes through *after* losing a loved one.

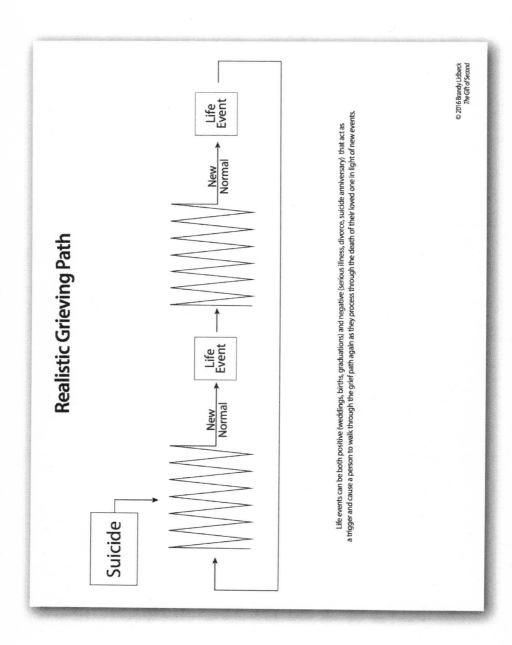

Realistic Grieving Path

Suicide

New Normal

Life Event

New Normal

Life Event

Life events can be both positive (weddings, births, graduations) and negative (serious illness, divorce, suicide anniversary) that act as a trigger and cause a person to walk through the grief path again as they process through the death of their loved one in light of new events.

© 2016 Brandy Lidbeck
The Gift of Second

Although the theory created by Kübler-Ross is strong and has merit, it gives the illusion that, at some point, grief is complete. We, as survivors, know the grief is never finished. The intensity lessens over time, and the consuming emotions become more stable, but grief is never fully complete. When folks expect their grief to end and their pain to be erased, they are, oftentimes, focused on an imaginary timeline, waiting for that magical day to wipe away their hurt and allow their life to resume as it was before this great tragedy. When we expect the impossible, we are always disappointed.

Grief is neither linear, nor does it adhere to a particular path. I created this image to depict the manner in which grief really affects us.

The Realistic Grieving Path begins with a suicide, causing a surviving individual to begin the grief process. The feelings one experiences are overwhelming, chaotic, erratic, and all-encompassing. I liken this feeling to the destruction of an earthquake. Not only does it rock our worlds and bring devastation to our lives, but it also creates cracks in our foundation, causing us to doubt all that was. The picture depicts waves of grief similar to an earthquake's seismic waves. One moment we can feel intense heart-ache and sadness, and then next moment we are full of anger and rage. Always unpredictable and never convenient, walking through grief can be unbearable much of the time.

As survivors work through their grief, they will eventually arrive at a phase titled 'New Normal.' New normal is labeled as such because we will never return to the person we were before the suicide. How could we? This phase becomes our new status quo, the phase in which we go about our days, no longer so consumed with grief. Life begins to carry on in this new normal stage until a 'life event' occurs. A life event can be positive, such as a wedding, the birth of a baby, or a graduation, or negative like the anniversary of the suicide, a serious illness, or a job loss. Regardless of the event, this scenario acts as a trigger and causes the survivor to walk through the grief path again as they process the death of their loved one once more in light of the new events.

As I prepared for my wedding, I thought very little of the absence of my mom for the ceremony. Nor did I think of her at all during the honeymoon. Upon returning from the honeymoon; however, while setting up house with my husband, something out of the blue, it seemed, occurred. Two days after returning, my husband and I sat down to make our first grocery list as a married couple. Every idea he had for meals seemed horrible, and I began to snap at him for each suggestion. Eventually, my wise husband asked, "What is the matter? Why are you so frustrated?" Without pause and without thinking, I began to sob. The only thing I could get out between deep crying breaths was, "My mom should have been at my wedding and she wasn't." To me, at the time, (and I am sure my husband as well) this seemed so odd and unexpected. In reality, it is a perfect example of a 'life event' as described above in the Realistic Grieving Path.

The wedding took place seventeen years after my mom's suicide and, leading up to the wedding, I had been relatively unaffected by her death as it pertained to wedding preparations. The major life event, though, rocked my world and caused me to walk through the process again as I mourned my mom missing my wedding.

The events do not need to be big; they can be small, such as running into an old friend you haven't seen in years who reminds you of your loved one or even simply hearing a song your loved one enjoyed. The idea is that events happen our entire lives, and many can trigger different parts within us to feel the loss of our loved one more fully. It is then that we must work through the death again. Walking through the grief path again by no means negates any grief work we have done before; instead, it brings to light different aspects that need more healing or attention. Grief is both cyclical and never-ending. We will never fully 'get over' the suicide of a loved one, and I believe this model best depicts the reality of grief. When discussing his son's suicide, Tony Dungy, former NFL Coach of the Indianapolis Colts, wrote in his book, *Quiet Strength: A Memoir*, "First, there is no typical grief cycle, and second, it's not something I went through. I'm still grieving."

When an individual has experienced such a tremendous loss as suicide, the entire body feels it. Symptoms of grief typically manifest as follows:

- Difficulty sleeping
- Loss of appetite
- Headaches
- Crying
- Aches and pains
- Anxiety
- Isolation
- Anger
- Guilt
- Sadness
- Fatigue
- Shock
- Depression

Each of these symptoms feels ever-present in the beginning, and the survivor may fear these feelings will consume them always. In time, though, these feelings will lessen in intensity and come in waves instead, often arising without warning. Eventually, feelings will surface with only a life trigger or memory of the loved one. Getting through will not always be so overwhelming. The grief path is normal and one to fully expect as you traverse life after suicide. We will never be 'over' the pain and devastation completely, but it won't always dictate our lives. There are times, however, when grieving individuals get stuck and are unable to move forward. This is called Complicated Grief, and we will discuss this more fully as it can often occur after a suicide.

Complicated Grief

Grief symptoms, with time, begin to lessen and eventually improve bit by bit. Complicated grief, however, is the opposite. For those experiencing complicated grief, the symptoms tend to get worse. If the symptoms listed above in typical grief do not begin to improve after six months, it could be considered complicated grief. According to the Mayo Clinic, "Complicated grief is like being in an ongoing, heightened state of mourning that keeps you from healing."

In their journal article in *World Psychiatry*, authors Sidney Zisook and Katherine Shear write,

> Bereaved individuals with complicated grief find themselves in a repetitive loop of intense yearning and longing that becomes the major focus of their lives, albeit accompanied by inevitable sadness, frustration, and anxiety. Complicated grievers may perceive their grief as frightening, shameful, and strange. They may believe that their life is over and that the intense pain they constantly endure will never cease. Alternatively, there are grievers who do not want the grief to end, as they feel it is all that is left of the relationship with their loved one. Sometimes, people think that, by enjoying their life, they are betraying their lost loved one.

If you have not seen any improvement in your grief and life still seems unbearable much longer than you expected, it is necessary to seek professional help as unaddressed, complicated grief will not get better with time. A therapist can help you walk through the grief in a healthy and productive manner. Because finding a trusted mental health provider can be daunting and overwhelming for many, I have devoted an entire chapter in this book on how to find the best therapist for you.

Remember, there is no timetable or limit to grief. Be kind to yourself. Do not compare your grief to others', as each individual person grieves each individual relationship differently. It is unique, and to shame yourself for not being 'farther along' in the grief process discounts the genuine feelings you have. Suicide is tragic, and we need to give ourselves permission to feel the enormity of all the emotions as they present themselves. I cannot tell you the number of times I have heard from other survivors (or even said myself), "I just need to move on and not have this affect me any longer. Other people seem to be handling this far better than I am." When our loved ones choose to die, we cannot shame ourselves for being impacted.

Many people fight grief and try not to let death affect them, as they believe showing emotions is weak. In *Traveling Mercies*, Anne Lamott writes,

> But what I've discovered since is that the lifelong fear
> of grief keeps us in a barren, isolated place and that
> only grieving can heal grief; the passage of time will
> lessen the acuteness, but time alone, without the di-
> rect experience with grief, will not heal it.

Grief Work

Many people fear working through the grief, expecting it will be too much to bear. They believe if they allow themselves to start crying, they may never be able to stop. And so, out of self-preservation, they refuse themselves the opportunity to grieve appropriately. They lock up all those feelings and emotions and avoid conversations pertaining to the death. Although they may feel they are protecting themselves, they are actually only injuring themselves further. When we do not grieve, the feelings do not simply go away. Instead, they simmer and boil beneath the surface until they can no longer be contained. When we prevent grief from naturally occurring, it is similar to pouring gasoline on a field of dead grass and shrubs. Eventually, an unexpected spark will come along and engulf the entire lot, leaving a blaze that is completely unmanageable. The repercussions of grief-avoidance are limitless. Not only does it impact our condition of life, it also impacts each succeeding generation. Substance abuse, broken relationships, mental illness, and suicide are just a few of the common consequences of unresolved grief.

The reality of working through grief: It is painful and exhausting. It's true. It is called 'grief work' because it is just that: work. So why do it? We must work through the grief because when we do, we find healing. When we allow ourselves the opportunity to fully feel the pain, trauma, sadness, anger, devastation, betrayal, and abandonment, without censor, we can then also fully experience healing. Healing brings peace, comfort, joy, and the ability to continue living a beautiful life. The grief work is painful, but it is also temporary. Resisting the work, however, has lifelong ramifications. When we are courageous enough to do grief work, we fully acknowledge our own worth and the value of our loved one, and we choose to be honest with the pain.

Questions to Consider

Have you experienced 'life events' that have acted as a trigger and caused you to move through the grief path again?

Does one feeling of grief seem more overwhelming or pertinent for you?

Have you felt shame or frustration you have not 'moved on' as quickly as others have in the grieving process? Do you think it is necessarily healthy or even possible to do so?

Do you think complicated grief is something you have experienced?

Do you have any feelings (good, bad, scary, shameful, embarrassed, etc.) about reaching out to a mental health professional to seek treatment?

What are your feelings about grief work? What do you think about the example of boiling water or a burning field as it pertains to avoided grief becoming too powerful to contain?

CHAPTER 2

Guilt and Shame

"Guilt is perhaps the most painful companion to death."

—ELISABETH KÜBLER-ROSS

TWO EMOTIONS TYPICALLY manifest after a loved one's suicide and negatively impact a survivor at the core of their existence. Guilt and shame can destroy an individual and, unfortunately, both are common after a suicide.

Guilt

Guilt is the belief we did not do enough to keep our loved ones here on Earth. Oftentimes, with guilt, we get stuck in 'if/then' thinking.

"If only I had known how he was feeling, then I could have helped him get the assistance he needed."

"If only I had come home an hour earlier, then she might still be alive today."

"If only I had paid more attention to the warning signs, then I could have prevented this."

If/Then thinking is the false belief that we had the power to prevent the suicide, and, because we failed to keep the person alive, we are to blame. This belief is typically self-imposed and always inaccurate. Most survivors discuss the shock they felt after their loved one's suicide. It's shocking because we never saw it coming. We cannot prevent something we don't see coming.

When my mom took her own life, my dad and brother were out of town, and my mom convinced me to go play elsewhere for the afternoon. She told me I could come home after 3:30. After I came home and discovered her lifeless body, I realized that evening that if I hadn't left the house that day, my mom would still be alive. When my dad returned home, one of the first things he said to me was probably the wisest statement he ever could have spoken to a young girl, "This was not your fault because you left the house. If you had stayed home she could have killed herself the next day or the next week or the next month. You cannot blame yourself at all for this." In that moment my dad spoke an incredible truth to me that, I believe, prevented any chance of guilt planting a seed in my mind. He didn't blame me because I was not to blame. He was right. My mom was strategic in getting me out of our home, but if her attempts at achieving an empty house that day failed, it might only have prolonged her life a short while.

If I had known she was going to kill herself, I would never have left. And you wouldn't have left either if you had known. Hear me on that one, friend; if we knew they were going to take their lives, we would have done everything possible to stop it. We cannot blame ourselves for unforesee-able events. Many survivors state they saw no signs their loved one was contemplating suicide but will often blame themselves for not doing more, saying more, or being more. Merriam-Webster defines 'guilt' as "feelings of culpability esp. for imagined offenses or from a sense of inadequacy." Survivors often carry an unrealistic and imagined sense of responsibility in the death of our loved one. In this imagined state of thinking, we be-lieve we are to blame for not preventing another person from ending their life, an action which we knew nothing about beforehand.

I know some of you reading this are thinking, "I should have known though because my loved one had attempted suicide before," or "They told me they were going to kill themselves, and I didn't believe it, so I did nothing to stop it." Still, some of you will say, "We had a fight right before he killed him-self; I am the reason he took his life." I understand all of these sentiments, I do, but, honestly, we cannot take responsibility for another's actions. In a survey I posted online, I received the following response from a fellow survivor who lost her child, "Do not shoulda, woulda, coulda. Remember that your child made a choice from free will. Remember that they died of mental illness."

I think we sometimes hold on to the guilt as our last sort of connection to our loved one. We often have a false belief that if we stop feeling guilty for not preventing the suicide, then we, by default, consent to it. It is simply not true. In one of the most beautiful pieces I have read on the subject of loss to suicide, LaRita Archibald writes in *Reinforcement in the Aftermath of Suicide*:

> To assume responsibility for this death, or to place responsibility upon another, robs the one who died of their personhood and invalidates the enormity of their pain and their desperate need for relief.

We cannot accept responsibility or assume guilt for our loved one's decision to end their life.

Shame

While guilt says we did not *do* enough to prevent the suicide, shame tells us we *are* not enough. Many survivors, especially children who have lost a parent to suicide, express feeling worthless or unlovable. The survivor takes on the belief that, if they were more valuable, then maybe their parent would not have *chosen* to permanently leave them by death. Surely, if my mom saw value in me, she would have chosen life, right? I wrestled with this for years. It wasn't until twenty-four years later that I realized my mom's suicide says nothing about my value or worth; it only speaks to her own mental state.

Suicide carries a massive stigma in society. Many survivors express feeling people will perceive them or their loved one who died as a 'freak' if they knew about the cause of death. And because of that, often, suicide is kept a secret. In the foreword of *Survivors of Suicide* by Albert C. Cain, Edwin Shneidman writes,

> I believe the person who commits suicide puts his psychological skeleton in the survivor's emotional closet—he sentences the

survivor to deal with many negative feelings and, more, to become obsessed with thoughts regarding his own actual or possible role in having precipitated the suicidal act or having failed to abort it. It can be a heavy load.

Many times after a suicide, the survivor believes they failed in some regard, failed as a protecting parent, a lovable child, a supportive spouse, a safe sibling, or a caring and listening friend. We believe that if we had been more approachable or more helpful, or if our loved one knew how much we truly loved them, then they wouldn't have been forced to choose death. We believe we failed and so we believe we *are* failures. We go through life shaming ourselves for not measuring up, not showing up, and truthfully, we shame ourselves for not being their Savior. We kick ourselves for not being everything our loved one needed to stay alive, and we blame ourselves for not keeping them alive. We carry the burden of a scarlet letter 'F' for Failure. We failed to protect and save our loved one because we were not enough.

I bought into this lie for far too long—decades, in fact. I believed all of the things mentioned above, and after several interviews and conversations with other survivors, I know I am not unique in this regard. We are not their Saviors, and to accept the responsibility of their choice to die is neither fair nor healthy. There is no other cause of death that wrecks the emotional psyche of a survivor quite like suicide. I have met people who lost a loved one to suicide forty years ago who still express feelings of guilt and shame. The emotional and physical toll this self-imposed blame takes on a survivor can be devastating. Countless survivors share that they have chronic health problems today, likely due to the stress of blame, shame, and guilt compounded over years.

Out of this entire book, there is no more important message that I want to share with you: You are not to blame, and you are enough. Our loved ones were sick. They were dealing with mental illness, they felt hopeless, and they believed their lives had no value. They were in an incredibly dark place which we could not penetrate. Professionals could not save them, medicine did not cure them, and love from others couldn't touch them. Their choice to die was their last solution to end the unimaginable physical and emotional pain they experienced every minute of every day. They were not intentionally trying to bring us pain but rather desperately trying to end their own. We will not condone suicide, but neither can we continue to take responsibility for it or allow it determine our own value.

If you have found yourself holding on to the shame and guilt after the suicide, I encourage you to ask yourself what you gain by continually blaming or hating yourself. We cannot change what took place, and by releasing the guilt and shame, we are allowing life to enter into our own bodies again. No longer in bondage to the self-blame, we are able to see fully the suicide for what it was: their attempt to end their pain. Unfortunately, accepting responsibility does not alter the outcome of their life; it only destroys ours.

Questions to Consider

Do you struggle with feelings of guilt, believing you could have done more to save your loved one or to prevent the suicide?

Do you struggle with shame? Do you feel less than, believing if you *were* more, your loved one might have had more reason to stay alive?

Have you struggled with how others will perceive you or your loved one if they discover the cause of death was suicide?

Why do you think feelings of guilt and shame are so prevalent among survivors?

Does this chapter allow you to entertain the idea you are not to blame for the suicide and your value is not determined by their suicide?

CHAPTER 3

Trauma and PTSD

"There are wounds that never show on the body that are deeper and more hurtful than anything that bleeds."

— LAURELL K. HAMILTON

As HUMANS, WE often have, on some level, a warning that death is imminent. Maybe a loved one is fighting a long battle with terminal cancer and we understand this illness will eventually take their life. Or, maybe we have an elderly relative who will likely pass due to natural causes. Regardless of how an individual we love and care for dies, death is always difficult to experience, and we feel a hole in our hearts moving forward. These types of deaths, however, afford us the opportunity to prepare ourselves and even to say goodbye. We will grieve their loss as we move onward, but our minds can wrap around the cause of death. Suicide is different--very different. Suicide is considered a traumatic loss.

Traumatic Loss is one that occurs without any warning and, often, involves a violent component. Typically, this involves a fatal accident, homicide, or suicide. Traumatic loss can be extremely difficult for those left behind because we are unprepared for the event, and we usually have no previous life experience with something as horrific as this from which to draw knowledge and healing. Suicide can leave surviving friends and family members with a great deal of psychological trauma. Some of the signs and symptoms of trauma include:

Physical:

- Insomnia
- Easily startled
- Hypervigilance
- Anxiety
- Fatigue
- Sexual dysfunction
- Irritability
- Eating too much or too little
- Physical muscle pain

Psychological:

- Shock
- Depression
- Anxiety
- Panic attacks
- Disbelief
- Fear
- Obsessive and compulsive behaviors (i.e. checking and rechecking doors and locks to give one's self a fleeting sense of security)
- Shame
- Guilt (not being able to prevent the suicide)
- Emotional numbing

Cognitive:

- Inability to concentrate
- Mood swings
- Memory loss

- Ongoing nightmares
- Intrusive thoughts
- Mental replaying of the event or of receiving news of the event over and over again
- Confusion

Behavioral:

- Lack of interest in activities that were once enjoyable
- Social withdrawal or isolation
- Increase in drug or alcohol consumption (or any other addictive substance or activity)

When a traumatic loss occurs, our entire sense of safety and security in this world is shattered and our innocence lost. We no longer have a safe worldview. We never, in our most horrific nightmares, could have imagined a loss quite like the suicide of our loved one. Unfortunately, for the survivors of suicide loss, we often face the grim reality of finding our loved one after they took their life. Many of us, including me, have come home and unexpectedly found our loved ones dead. Or worse, many of us have been present when someone took his or her own life and we witnessed the actual event. Memories of this traumatic event stay in our minds, and we replay them over and over again. I was unable to remember what my mom looked like for years without first looking at a picture. Instead, the only image I could recall of my mom was the one I found that afternoon in our home, which looked nothing like her living self.

It is normal to experience the symptoms of trauma listed above for the first month, but if these symptoms last longer than one month, it could be more serious, like Post Traumatic Stress Disorder (PTSD). We have all heard the term a million times, but like a fellow survivor told me in an interview, "I had no idea I could have PTSD from finding my dad after he killed himself. I thought PTSD was only something you got after being shot at in Iraq."

A large number of fellow survivors I have spoken with have downplayed their symptoms because they were either unaware their symptoms were more serious or they felt ashamed and embarrassed they couldn't just 'get over' the trauma of finding their loved one. So, instead of reaching out for help, they continue to unnecessarily suffer. Here is a list of questions to ask yourself as it pertains to the symptoms of PTSD.

Do you have continued thoughts or memories related to the event?

Do you have recurring dreams about the event?

Do you have flashbacks of the trauma?

Do you have a difficult time when anything triggers a memory of the event?

Do you try to avoid thinking about the trauma or avoid memories of it?

Do you try to avoid people, places, conversations, objects, or activities that are associated with the trauma?

Do you have a difficult time remembering details of the trauma?

Do you have negative beliefs about yourself, such as 'I am bad' or 'people are untrustworthy'?

Do you blame yourself for the trauma?

Are you in a continued state of feeling guilt, shame, anger, fear, or horror?

Do you have less interest in activities you used to enjoy?

Do you find it difficult to experience love, joy, happiness, and satisfaction?

Do you have difficulty sleeping?

Do you have difficulty concentrating?

Do you have anger outbursts?

Are you in a constant state of worrying about something bad happening?

Do you behave recklessly or engage in self-destructive behavior?

Did you answer 'yes' to many of these questions? If some of the above questions resonate, it is important to seek professional help. As much as we would love to believe these signs will disappear with time, the reality is the opposite. As time progresses, and without proper treatment, the symptoms will only intensify. These indicators will eventually make it difficult to even function in life. Far too often, with suicide, a level of shame enters into our being, we stop talking about it and begin to isolate from others. Once we isolate, we have little to no resources in place, and life becomes unnecessarily difficult for the survivor. There is help available, though, and it is critical to seek it out. Recognize there is no shame in needing help. Often, the survivor becomes angry or sad their loved one did not seek help from family or professionals, but when it is time for us to seek help, we dismiss the need for assistance and suffer alone. A licensed psychologist or therapist, trained in trauma work and with a great understanding of PTSD, can dramatically improve a client's life by working through the trauma with them. See the Therapy and Groups chapter for a full explanation of therapists and services available.

My colleague, Margy Grebe, a licensed marriage and family therapist who works with clients experiencing PTSD described it as follows:

> When trauma of this nature occurs, we are often unable to put the memory of what happened into our history. In other words, we relive the event as if it is present instead of in the past. The pictures in our minds, the feelings we experienced both physically and emotionally, and the negative cognitive messages we experienced (i.e. it's my fault, I should have done something different/better/more, I'm not safe, I'm not valuable enough to live for, etc.), break into our lives via flashbacks or nightmares of the event, seemingly disconnected body memories, and feeling as if the event is happening again/still in the now. We can get stuck in our minds and our body's re-experiencing of what happened and sometimes not even know what has triggered us to see, feel, and/or act like the event is present.

The important part to recognize, as Margy points out, is that most of the time we are completely unaware of what caused our flashbacks and memories but our minds and bodies are being continually re-traumatized, sometimes to an even greater scale than the original event. It doesn't need to be like this. Most of the time, if an individual attends specific treatment pertaining to trauma, people with PTSD can work through it completely without any lingering traumatizing flashbacks or invasive memories at all.

Experiencing PTSD from Afar

Every day I hear fellow survivors remark they still replay, in their minds, the event of finding their loved one dead after the suicide or even receiving the phone call informing them their loved one had died. The survivors explain they are unable to stop thinking about it: their minds and bodies are subconsciously and endlessly running through the trauma. Both of these highlight classic PTSD symptoms. When we find ourselves re-experiencing the trauma time and time again in our minds, it is as if we are stuck, unable to leave the scene, and our bodies force us to live through it continually and without warning. The important thing to realize is we do not need to be present at the scene of the suicide nor do we need to see graphic images in person to be traumatized. Sometimes individuals are traumatized by merely learning of the death over the phone or in the newspaper.

Most of us can easily recall where we were on the morning of September 11, 2001 and how we learned of the terrorist attacks against the USA. We saw horrible images on TV that showed destruction, ruin, evil, and the loss of life. For the people in those buildings, planes, and streets that day, the personal trauma was unbearable. Many individuals watching the prolonged news coverage from their living room TV's in far-away places were equally traumatized by what they saw on the screen and experienced PTSD in the aftermath. Even though they were not intimately impacted by the attacks, they still found it necessary to seek treatment for their PTSD symptoms because of simply seeing and hearing of the attacks. I say this to convey the point that we can be traumatized by events even from afar. So, if you are looking at the questions above and feel that some resonate strongly with you as it pertains to your loved one's suicide, even if you were not actually present at the scene, I encourage you to seek help.

The trauma of a suicide does not end the day we bury our loved ones. Like the water in a ripple effect after a stone has been tossed in, we continually feel and experience the consequences of that stone in our lives. To deny the impact is to deny ourselves.

Questions to Consider

Do you find it hard to stop thinking about the day and events surrounding your loved one's death?

When answering the questions related to PTSD, do you feel some of them resonate in your life today? If so, which ones do you relate to the most?

Have you started accepting the intrusive thoughts, bad dreams, and flashbacks as just something you will 'have to live with' from now on? Would you like to be free of these symptoms?

Do you experience any level of shame or embarrassment that you cannot 'just get over it' or 'stop thinking about it'? (If you do, please recognize there is no shame and there is nothing to be embarrassed of. The body's natural defense against something so scary is to protect itself and, sometimes, we get stuck and need a little help in getting un-stuck).

CHAPTER 4

Therapy and Groups

"Death by suicide is not a gentle deathbed gathering; it rips apart lives and beliefs and sets its survivors on a prolonged and devastating journey."

—KAY REDFIELD JAMISON

I FOUGHT THE idea of therapy my entire life, believing that anyone needing to go was weak. After a few life events occurred which triggered some strong feelings about my mom, and with some coaxing from a co-worker, I agreed to enter into therapy and really discuss my mom's suicide for the first time, thirteen years after her death. Scared, anxious, embarrassed, and cautious, I entered the therapist's office. Hoping I could be there for just a session or two until I was 'all better,' I had a conversation with my therapist that looked like this:

> Me: How long do you think this will take? How many sessions will I have to be here?
> Therapist (shaking her head): Um, there's no way to know right now.
> Me: Give me a ballpark timeframe. A month? Two months?
> Therapist: Oh no, it will be for quite a while.
> Me: (heavy sigh)

Although I didn't like the therapist's answer, I agreed to go weekly. I had seen how thirteen years of refusing to talk about my mom's suicide had taken its toll on me physically, emotionally, and spiritually. Originally,

I thought I would discuss only her suicide, but the reality is I walked in with my protective walls built high which were causing crumbling in other areas of my life. I had built a fortress around me, defending myself from others so that I would never again experience the tremendous pain I had with my mom. I had, therefore, siphoned off the ability to feel and express true, raw emotions. I didn't trust anyone, I refused to cry (it was another sign of weakness, I believed), and I was trying to pretend my mom's suicide had no effect on me. I was unaware of it, but my mom's death had power over me despite my constant attempts to pretend I was not bothered by it. I looked 'fine' on the outside, but on the inside I was a fragile woman desperate for healing.

Many people reading this book also believe, as I originally did, that (1) to attend therapy is a sign of weakness and (2) therapy is unnecessary and we can handle this on our own. The reality is, we can't. We are ill-equipped and incapable of processing the magnitude of a suicide. With the suicide of our loved one we have experienced a distressing, traumatic, chaotic, and forever life-altering and unnecessary death. How could we ever assume we could process this alone and solely within the confines of our own mind?

I often thought the only people who attended therapy were noticeably distraught and not strong enough to figure out life on their own. They were failures who needed their hands held. Allow me to paint a different picture if you have assumed the same. When I entered into therapy, I had countless friends, I was always the life of the party, I had completed my bachelor's degree, and I was attending classes for my master's. I graduated from both with honors. I had no substance or alcohol addiction, I never cried, and I never thought twice about my mom's suicide. I was successful and appeared to be winning at life. The reality is therapy is not for the weak; instead, I have learned, therapy is for the courageous.

I hadn't grieved my mom's suicide; I only stuffed it deep down and refused to look at it. To assume the effects of her death would go away in time and on their own was a huge disservice to myself. Psychologist Robert Kavanaugh writes:

Deposits of unfinished grief reside in more American hearts than I ever imagined. Until these pockets are opened and their contents aired openly, they block unimagined amounts of human growth and potential. They can give rise to bizarre and unexplained behavior which causes untold internal stress.

This chapter serves as a tool on how therapy works. I want to assist you in finding help while also reducing the shame and stigma attached to therapy as a whole. We will discuss how to find a qualified therapist who best fits your need and how to navigate insurance and payment. We will also have a discussion of therapy specific to trauma and grief and support groups.

Finding a Qualified Therapist

The first hurdle survivors often face is where to start. It is incredibly difficult even to know where to begin and, in the face of grief, it can be overwhelming. Finding a good therapist can be done in several ways. First, ask a friend or family member if they could recommend a therapist they have seen in the past. Personal referral is usually one of the best approaches because the therapist is being referred to you by someone who found them helpful. Second, check with your insurance provider. Your insurance company can give you a list of therapists in your local area who are covered under your plan. This one, unfortunately, may not always provide the best therapists (like your friend or family referral), but it could give you a great starting place. Third, great online resources are available to help you, such as therapists.psychologytoday.com. On the website, you can search by zip code to find therapists in your area and scan their profiles to determine if they would be a good match. The list is not exhaustive but is a great starting place.

When looking for therapists, it is important to look for a few key words specific to the type of work they specialize in. Most therapists have a website which will describe the type of clients they generally see (men, women, adults, children) and different areas they are trained in and focus on (anxiety, addiction, grief). When searching for a therapist after a suicide, look for one that specializes in grief and trauma. Often, the feelings we have such as anxiety and depression are a result of unresolved grief, so having a trained therapist walk us through the grief can help to naturally lessen the other symptoms we are experiencing.

When you find a therapist who seems to match your preferred location and specialization, call the therapist. Explain to them why you are seeking counseling and what you want help with. You can get a good feel for a therapist in that first conversation, and the therapist can also tell you if they feel qualified to work with you and, if not, give you a referral of someone better suited for your needs. A referral from another therapist is gold! They are not going to refer clients or potential clients to someone they do not feel is competent. For example, sometimes I get calls from potential clients looking for a therapist to help their child with an eating disorder. I do not feel equipped to work effectively in this area, so I would refer them to a colleague I know and trust that specializes in eating disorders. This is standard in the mental health profession.

During that first phone conversation and also the first session, it is important to treat it like an interview. Think of it as interviewing the therapist to see whether they will be a good fit for you both professionally and personally. If you do not feel comfortable or safe with them for one reason or another, it is okay to ask them for a referral of another therapist that may suit your needs better. This is also standard in the mental health profession. If you feel uncomfortable doing this, remember that you are there to get help. You will be wasting your time and money if you continue to see a therapist you are not comfortable with. If you tell the therapist you would like a referral to another professional, they will have no issue referring you on. Sometimes it just doesn't work out. If, for some reason, the therapist has an issue with you switching to a new therapist, this may be a good confirmation they are not a good fit for you. A therapist should not try to get a client to stay despite her discomfort. Our motto is 'Do No Harm.'

If, however, you have interviewed countless therapists and still are unable to find a good match despite qualified therapists available in your area, I would challenge you to examine your level of willingness and readiness to seek therapy. Sometimes we are just not ready to enter into the difficult work of grief and that is okay. If you notice resistance within yourself, it is okay to slow down and revisit the issue when you feel the time is right.

How to Pay for Therapy

If you have health insurance that provides mental health services, it can be a huge blessing to utilize this benefit. Make sure your therapist is covered under your plan, but expect to still be responsible for a co-pay or any charges until your deductible is met. Sometimes, for one reason or another, a therapist does not accept insurance. In a situation like this, the therapist can provide you with a receipt which you, in turn, can provide to your insurance company for a reimbursement. It is important to check with your insurance company first to see if reimbursement is available. Also, sometimes benefits through an employer will include an Employee Assistance Program (EAP), which will allow for clients to receive a predetermined amount of counseling sessions for free. Typically, this number is about six. Although six sessions are not enough to do a real amount of work, it is a good starting point and worth looking into.

If you do not have insurance or wish not to use it, cash is an option. The therapist and you will agree upon a rate, and you will be expected to pay it at the time of service unless another arrangement has been made. Therapy can be expensive, and sometimes it is out of our budget. Ask your therapist if they work on a sliding scale. Therapists and agencies will often give a client a discounted rate dependent on the need of the client. A therapist wants a client to receive the help they need and not be turned away due to the inability to pay. If, for some reason, the therapist is unable to offer a discounted price or is unable to see you at a rate that works within your budget, ask the therapist if he or she could refer you to a non-profit agency. A non-profit agency can usually provide services at a low cost to the client. Another option is seeing a therapist intern or trainee. When therapists first finish graduate school, before they can become licensed, they are required to gain a significant number of practical hours under the supervision of a licensed therapist who guides them in the direction to take clients. Interns and trainees see clients for a fraction of the cost of licensed therapists (sometimes charging only $10 per session), but because they are required to seek supervision from a licensed therapist in each client case, the client, in essence, gets two therapists for the price of one. Interns are never as experienced as a licensed therapist, but they can serve as a great resource if funds are limited.

In order for a therapist to collect payment from an insurance provider, they must first provide a diagnosis of the client to illustrate the need for this person to receive services and, in turn, for insurance to pay for it. Unfortunately, this diagnosis stays with you for life. If, perhaps, you entered into therapy majorly depressed and were rightfully diagnosed as such by your therapist, but then through treatment and possibly medication found incredible improvement, the diagnosis will still be on your record. If you pay cash, however, this diagnosis will not be disclosed to your insurance provider. It's something to think about before moving forward. I strongly encourage clients to get the help they need regardless of this scenario, but some people are unaware insurance companies operate this way with mental health, and it is best to let you make an informed decision.

What Type of Therapy is Best for Me?

The best type of therapy for you is what works, what you prefer, and what yields the results you are seeking. Let's look at a variety of therapies that could be beneficial. All of the therapies mentioned below would be helpful to survivors of suicide loss.

Individual Therapy is just how it sounds: individual. A client and a therapist meet one-on-one to discuss whatever the client would like to work on. This setting, I believe, is best for an individual to work through the feelings and emotions without having to censor them. Sometimes, for example, in family therapy, clients might not want to speak openly and honestly about how they are feeling if they fear it will upset another family member present in the room. In individual therapy, though, the client is afforded the opportunity to candidly speak with the therapist about their pain, emotions, struggles, conflict, and grief without censorship. This is a gift!

Trauma Therapy is an integral part of the grief process for survivors of suicide loss. Trauma and PTSD do not go away just by talking about them. A therapist who is trained in EMDR (Eye Movement Desensitization and Reprocessing) therapy (a specific approach to trauma and PTSD) could be an essential part of your grief work. I would strongly suggest you find a therapist trained in EMDR if the Trauma and PTSD chapter in this book resonates with you. The therapist can better explain how it works and if you would be a good candidate for this type of therapy. Some therapists are specifically trained in trauma work, and they would also be a good match.

Family Therapy can be helpful after a suicide. Typically, family therapy includes just the immediate family, but more members can be added if the therapist and clients mutually agree it would be beneficial. Family therapy allows all family members to be in the same place at the same time to process the incredible loss. It is beneficial because it allows dialogue to be opened among the family and for all members to safely share their experience and feelings under the care of a trained therapist. The therapist can help guide conversation and give the family a set of tools for how to care for and support one another moving forward.

Survivors of Suicide Groups can be worth their weight in gold. The endless benefits one gets from sharing with and listening to other survivors is priceless. Survivors often feel alone and isolated and these groups can help survivors feel understood, connected, hopeful, and encouraged. Sometimes these groups are run by a licensed therapist for a fee and other times there are peer-run support groups free of charge. Peer groups are led by survivors. This is an invaluable resource. If you can find one near you, I would strongly encourage it.

Children's Therapy will not look like that of an adult's. Sometimes the children are too young to fully understand death and loss, and other times they cannot cognitively process it. Thus, therapy must afford the child the opportunity to process the death and trauma when they cannot fully articulate their thoughts and feelings. Children process best through art and play. Art therapy allows children to comfortably express emotions through markers and paint, for example, when words are more difficult. A trained art therapist can help process the picture with the child and work through some of the themes presented in the art. Play therapy allows for grief work to take place as well but allows children to do it in the manner they are best at: play! If a therapist is merely talking with a child, it is likely not much benefit will result. A child needs to play and be creative in session. There are grief groups for children, though, and those are worth looking into. If a child is able to meet with peers that understand them fully and allow them to express their grief, while not feeling so unique and alone, it can be incredibly powerful.

Marilyn Koenig, founder of Friends for Survival, (discussed in the resources chapter) told me once, "We're going to grieve the same way we lived." By this, she meant that those who avoided talking about feelings and emotions before the suicide grieved in the same avoidant manner after. Folks who got through life by drinking alcohol to numb out those uncomfortable feelings would again reach for the bottle after the suicide. The pain of a suicide is unimaginable and to assume we can do it alone, in a healthy manner, is not realistic.

Therapy, on the outside, can seem daunting, expensive, and even confusing. I hope, in this chapter, I was able to show you otherwise. Therapy really is a gift to all those who will accept it. When we learn to process life in healthy and productive ways, we pass on that health and wisdom to our families. We are then able to break destructive cycles and learn appropriate coping and grieving skills, which sets us up for handling life as it occurs. The benefits of therapy can help bring healing to you and your future generations.

I will leave you with this wisdom from Fred Rogers, better known by his TV name, Mr. Rogers:

> Anything that's human is mentionable, and anything that is mentionable can be more manageable. When we can talk about our feelings, they become less overwhelming, less upsetting, and less scary. The people we trust with that important talk can help us know that we are not alone.

Questions to Consider

Have you ever felt therapy was only for weak people who are unable to 'get over it'?

Do you feel you could benefit from working with a therapist?

Does a support group of fellow survivors seem like something you would be willing to try?

Has the cost of therapy been a deterrent to you in the past? Do you think speaking with a therapist about lower fees is something you would be willing to look into?

CHAPTER 5

Communicating About Suicide

"For some moments in life there are no words."

—WILLY WONKA AND THE CHOCOLATE FACTORY

NO FORM OF death brings about more opportunity for awkward, uncomfortable, and hurtful conversations than that of a suicide. From both my personal experience as well as the responses from surveys and interviews with other survivors, it is clear there is no easy formula for how to proceed with dialogue pertaining to the cause of death. In this chapter, I hope to set the groundwork and offer some suggestions so that you may be better prepared in handling communication and dialogue as it pertains to suicide.

Almost immediately following my mom's suicide, I began to get questions from people pertaining to the exact nature of her death. Since I was the one who found my mom's body after she took her life, I received countless questions that were completely inappropriate. "How did she kill herself? What did the body look like? Where was she when she died?" In addition to questions specifically related to the condition of her body, I also received questions related to the suicide in general. Countless survivors of suicide loss echoed this experience as they explained the absurd number of questions they also received. "Did you know they were going to kill themselves? Did you know they were depressed? Did they leave you a note, and what did it say?" The questions are never ending when it comes to suicide. I call this 'Morbid Curiosity.'

Morbid Curiosity is a term I created in my twenties to describe all of the inappropriate questions people feel they have the freedom to ask a survivor. Maybe it's a good story for them to hear or maybe it's a form of control, trying to determine if they are susceptible to a suicide in their family by determining the warning signs we missed from our own experience. Regardless, the truth is that what is an entertaining story for them to hear is the worst day of our lives for us. I learned early on about this morbid curiosity, so I decided never to share about the suicide at all. In fact, I allowed most of my classmates to believe my parents were divorced so I did not have to discuss the truth and face the painful questions.

Why did I tell you all of this? Because I am not alone in my experience. Almost every single person I have interviewed or surveyed has conveyed a similar experience or what they call 'The deer in the headlights look.' Many survivors explained they have been more than willing and even desiring to talk about the death with others, but once they tell another individual their loved one died by suicide, the unsuspecting person becomes awkwardly quiet and just stares, as they have no idea how to proceed. Several survivors explained how other people become so awkward with the news of a suicide that the survivor has found themselves offering comfort to the other individual instead. One survivor mentioned that she strongly desires to keep the memory of her husband alive by talking about him with others, but due to the uncomfortable and awkward responses she has received, she feels she cannot.

Deciding how and what you will tell strangers and acquaintances regarding the nature of your loved one's death is entirely up to you. You must do something you feel comfortable with and that allows you to also practice self-care. I felt it was more damaging to tell folks and so, for the sake of my own well-being, I told no one. Others, in contrast, want others to know in hopes of keeping their loved one's memory alive and potentially reducing the stigma of suicide. How do you know what is best for you? Trial and error, I believe. Some survivors explained that if an individual asks them how their loved one died, the survivor will answer matter-of-factly and succinctly, "They died by suicide," and then continue on in the conversation, allowing no room for probing questions or inappropriate comments. Others explained they have no issue with the probing questions and actually enjoy becoming an open book about the topic to others.

When others ask probing questions, it can be painful, shaming, and overall difficult. Some survivors explained that they came up with a rehearsed script for responding to questions to allow themselves the opportunity to stay in control of the conversation and only share what they felt was safe for them. This, I feel, is a good practice. It might seem a bit fake, but the reality is, our first priority is to share only what feels safe to us. Remember, when being asked questions, we get to decide how little or how much we disclose. If someone asks us an inappropriate question, we have the freedom to answer, "I don't feel comfortable discussing this with you." I don't think people are out to cause harm; I simply believe most people do not think before they speak, and we are on the receiving end of their ignorance.

Suicide Conversations Within Family

Everything mentioned in this chapter so far is geared more toward strangers and acquaintances. Sometimes the hardest people to talk about suicide with, though, are those we know the best. How do we proceed with family? This one becomes tricky for several reasons. Family rules (how families relate to one another through spoken or unspoken rules) tend to dictate how we respond to life in general. When a suicide occurs, it can cause those family rules to set up some very harmful and destructive scenarios in the lives of survivors. Numerous survivors explained their family kept the cause of death a secret from other family members in an attempt to 'protect' them or to avoid family drama. This, I firmly believe, should never be the way to proceed. Apart from children (which we will discuss later in this chapter), there is no reason for people to withhold the truth from another family member. It is deceptive and robs that individual of grieving the loss in a healthy and honest manner. Folks may decide, "She wouldn't be able to handle knowing it was a suicide" or "It would destroy him to know," but this is not really a choice we get to make on someone else's behalf. Will it be horrible and devastating and earth-shattering for them to know the truth? Absolutely. But then we talk about it, we grieve, we get help, we reach out for support, and we accept it as truth. To be robbed of this opportunity because someone else thought it was in their 'best interest' is unfair and inappropriate. How would you feel if you believed your loved one died in an accident only to find out years later the suicide has actually been a family secret in an attempt to protect you? You would likely feel betrayed, deceived, and angry. You might also need to start your own grieving process all over again as you process the actual suicide for the first time. Please don't lie to other family members about it. And, if you have already lied about it, I strongly encourage you to go back now and tell the truth. We cannot control how others will respond to the news of a suicide, but it is best to be honest from day one.

Talking with Kids

What about kids? Do kids need to know it was a suicide? Can they process the knowledge of a suicide? Shouldn't we protect them? The answer to all of those questions is yes! Children need to know it was a suicide. Carla Fine, the author of *No Time to Say Goodbye*, interviewed Dr. Edward Dunne in her book regarding how to proceed with children. He said,

> It is unrealistic to hide the fact of suicide from children. Children eventually find out the truth and often under circumstances when they are given little support, like hearing the news from a schoolmate or a relative, for example. Children can pick up overtones in a family and can sense when something is not quite right. Why betray the trust of children when they've already been betrayed by one adult? Children should learn from the experience that not all adults will abandon you or let you down.

I love this wisdom because it is so true. These children have already been betrayed by one adult they loved, trusted, and depended on. To deceive and betray them again is unfathomable!

If your child is younger, say less than twelve, I don't think discussing the suicide is a great option at this point. But, in the future, it will need to be a priority. When discussing the suicide with a child, it is important to take their age into consideration. You will share less with a young child and more with an older one. As the child gets older though, it is important the discussion grows as well. Graphic details are unnecessary and will likely only scare the child, but keeping the focus on the state of mind of the one who died might be more beneficial. Some survivors have shared how they explained to their child that the loved one had an "illness in their brain that caused them to make a really bad choice to end their life." They then explained that the remaining family members don't have this same illness and will not leave them. Children worry that others will die as well, so it is vital to continually reassure kids that you will not die by suicide. It is key to keep the dialogue open and honest and allow your kids the opportunity to discuss it with you any time they have a question or concern.

One woman contacted me during the writing of this book and shared that she told her eleven-year-old daughter, at the time of her husband's suicide, that he died in an accident. Now, at age 15, she fears her daughter is too sensitive to know the truth and doesn't feel it is something she ever wants to disclose because suicide has such a 'stigma in our culture.' What better way to reduce a stigma than to openly discuss and dialogue about the suicide? Keeping a suicide hidden in the dark and under a blanket of deceit does nothing but reinforce the stigma. Openly discussing the suicide in an honest and safe manner with our kids allows for healthy grieving and growth.

Children's grief does not look like that of an adult. While a child may go run and play outside with his friends, it does not mean that he is 'handling it well.' It simply means he is playing outside with his friends. Conversely, you may see your child acting out, disobeying, failing school, or getting into trouble, all more obvious signs your child needs some help to work through the suicide. A child needs to process a suicide just as much as adults do. I talk about children's therapy in depth in the therapy chapter, and I encourage you to have your children meet with a therapist. It may be for just a short season or it may be for a longer one. It may even be for a time now and then again years down the road. Keeping the dialogue open will only help your child become a healthy adult.

It is my hope we can open the dialogue regarding suicide. Giving yourself permission as to the specific information you choose to share, the details you disclose, and the responses you want to have are all a part of self-care. Recognizing that people will say hurtful and ignorant statements is important, but how you choose to respond is the only part you can control. Openly and honestly discussing the suicide within your family is crucial. Family secrets of this magnitude will only destroy trust and relationships down the road. It's not worth it in the name of 'protecting' others. It is far better to share the truth and then, as a family, get the help you need to process the trauma and pain of it all. There is no shame in getting help but there is always shame in secrets. Secrets form and remain out of shame. Shame and secrets only perpetuate the stigma of suicide.

Questions to Consider

Have you experienced people asking you intrusive or hurtful questions? Have you figured out a level of answers that feels safe and comfortable for you to share?

Have you or your family decided to keep the suicide a secret from another person in order to 'protect' them from the truth? If so, did this chapter open up some reasons for you to consider telling them the truth instead?

Have you avoided talking about the suicide with children because they seem 'resilient' or you fear you may upset them by bringing it up?

Does the stigma of suicide prevent you from sharing the truth with others like it did for me in my younger years?

CHAPTER 6

What Helped Other Survivors

"You cannot stop the birds of sorrow from flying over your head, but you can stop them nesting in your hair."

—Eva Ibbotson, *The Dragonfly Pool*

When survivors were asked, "What helped you make it through this devastating loss?" four answers were common among all surveys and interviews. People were adamant about these answers and some even responded with, "If I didn't have____, I would not have made it through."

Finding Other Survivors

The first answer that came up repeatedly was, "I found another survivor to talk with who fully understood me like nobody else in my life could." Some mentioned they had a friend who had also experienced a suicide in their life, and they were able to talk with them to help sort through the emotions and feelings. Most, however, stated they attended a group for those impacted by suicide. It was in those rooms, they explained, they were able to receive comfort, understanding, acceptance, hope, and love and start to lessen the amount of guilt and shame they carried. Survivor groups are wonderful because they are mixed groups of individuals that usually would not be connected in the outside world, but inside those walls, they offer healing to one another.

Elizabeth Gilbert, author of *Eat, Pray, Love*, writes:

> Deep grief sometimes is almost like a specific location, a
> coordinate on a map of time. When you are standing in
> that forest of sorrow, you cannot imagine that you could
> ever find your way to a better place. But if someone can as-
> sure you that they themselves have stood in that same place,
> and now have moved on, sometimes this will bring hope.

Suicide-specific groups tend to fully understand the dynamics of suicide and what the survivor faces emotionally. There are survivor groups
listed in the resource chapter in this book, and I encourage you to check
one out in your area. If one does not exist, you can contact one of the
groups listed and ask for help to start one in your city. These groups
are peer led, and although some training is required to ensure safety for
all members within a meeting, there is no reason a group could not be
started in your own area. If you are looking for a meeting in your city
but none exists, I guarantee someone else in your neighborhood is looking for one as well. Meetings really only need two participants in order
for an individual to feel connected. If a suicide-specific group is not an
option, feel free to attend a general grief group. General groups can
typically be found most everywhere and although they are not specific
to suicide, they do focus on grief, loss, and self-care which are beneficial
regardless of the cause of death. In *The Sacred and Profane Love Machine*,
Iris Murdoch wrote, "Bereavement is a darkness impenetrable to the
imagination of the unbereaved." We cannot expect those who have not
experienced this pain to understand the depth of it. Suicide survivor
groups can be priceless.

Therapy
Many survivors expressed how necessary and beneficial therapy was for
them. Some only participated for a short duration while others attended
much longer, but all those who were able to work with a therapist described

it as invaluable. In *Epilogue*, Ann Roiphe penned, "Grief is in two parts. The first is loss. The second is the remaking of life." Therapy affords the client the remaking of life after a disturbing loss like suicide.

Some survivors explained they went to a therapist initially and gained nothing from it but later found a new therapist who was able to help begin the healing process for the survivor. Sometimes therapy is not helpful if (1) we attended therapy too early when we were not yet fully able to begin the process or (2) the therapist was not a good fit. As discussed in the Therapy and Groups chapter, finding a therapist you are comfortable with is critical. I cannot emphasize enough the value of therapy for me both personally and professionally. Author Gail Sheehy wrote, "People in grief need someone to walk with them without judging them." A therapist can do exactly that.

Service

Survivors named service as one of the most helpful ways to make it through the wreckage of suicide. When we are able to fully understand the depths of pain and suffering, we can offer ourselves to others facing the same turmoil. Three specific ways to serve others were listed repeatedly.

Suicide Prevention: Countless survivors mentioned getting involved in suicide prevention in many different forms. Some increase awareness by organizing walks and runs in memory of their loved one. They help raise funds to help educate the community on suicide risks, signs, and resources. Others mentioned getting involved with organizations such as American Foundation for Suicide Prevention whose mission is, "Save lives and bring hope to those affected by suicide."

Survivors of Suicide Loss Groups: Many people started a grief group, like the ones mentioned above, in their own area to assist other survivors experiencing the same pain. They felt their time and energy devoted to helping others who know the destruction first hand had been essential for their own healing. These survivors appreciated how they were able to be a lifeline to others while still maintaining connections in the group setting.

Speaking: A large number of people also shared they have become the face of suicide loss as they travel around speaking to an array of audiences. Some speakers talk with teens and share the incredible loss they experienced after their child took their own life in hopes of encouraging young adults to seek help if they have thoughts of suicide themselves. Others speak to state and local elected officials in a more formal setting in order to help raise awareness and support for those with mental illness. Still others will speak at conferences for survivors of suicide loss, providing emotional support. Regardless of the approach one takes in raising awareness of suicide, reducing the stigma is key. Until our society can talk about it openly and without shame, there will never be enough resources available for either the prevention side nor the postvention.

Serving others and giving back to the suicide community are great ways to also help yourself. Not only does it allow you to connect with others who can fully understand you, but it also can give you a sense of purpose and help lessen your own depression. Serving others allows us the opportunity to get outside of ourselves and love others, which in turn helps us love ourselves. It is important to note, though, the benefit of doing your own grief work before service to others, especially if the form of service is facilitating a grief group. If we have not done our own grieving, it is difficult to help others in their journey when our emotions are still so raw and bleeding.

I highly recommend serving others in any of the above outlets as a way of bringing good and healing to others in light of such a shattering loss.

God and Faith

Many survivors explained that faith in God was the only thing that got them through the suicide. They conveyed that continuing to trust God during this trauma was sometimes difficult but always necessary. Some stated that although it sounds cliché to a grieving individual, this passage from the Bible resonated profoundly: Proverbs 3:5 reads, "Trust in the LORD with all your heart, and lean not on your own understanding." The next chapter is entirely dedicated to God and faith, which I hope will offer some comfort to you.

Conclusion

Most people, when grieving, want to know two things specifically: 1) "When will this pain end?" and 2) "How am I going to make it through this?" Since creating *The Gift of Second*, a website for those impacted by the suicide of a loved one, I have been asked countless times, "What does the name of the website (and now this book) mean?" My answer is this: When an individual experiences a suicide, they are lost, devastated, and confused. They are in shock and have no idea where to even start. The website, through videos and blogs created by other survivors, offers support, encouragement, hope, and connection to others. The gift of going second is that there have been others before you who know and have experienced the same pain. They are able to come alongside you and say, "me too." It is the gift of going second, behind others who have been where you stand today. It is because of this I wanted to share what others found helpful in their journey so that you, too, will find comfort and healing.

Questions to Consider

What has been the most helpful to you during this difficult season?

Do any of the above mentioned items seem of interest to you?

Do you think serving other survivors could also benefit you as well as them?

Does the idea of starting a survivor group seem overwhelming or something you would actually be interested in doing?

Is there anything else not mentioned that you feel has been the most helpful for you?

CHAPTER 7

Incomprehensible Death

"In most cases, suicide is a solitary event and yet it has often far-reaching repercussions for many others. It is rather like throwing a stone into a pond; the ripples spread and spread."

—ALISON WERTHEIMER

AFTER A SUICIDE, survivors often find themselves living in rewind. Constantly, we look back for clues indicating the suicide was imminent. We replay past conversations and dissect our loved one's actions to determine what we missed. Could I have prevented it? How did I not see this coming? What did I miss? In the book, *A Healing Touch*, Susan Sterling writes the following:

> Even if those who take their own lives feel they have no choice—indeed, they often tragically believe their family and friends will be better off without them—the death rarely appears inevitable to those left behind. Feelings of anger and guilt and abandonment invade them, as if love should or could have prevented what happened. Survivors relive, over and over, the last days and months, even years, before the suicide, seeing now the signs that were missed, which they believe they should have recognized.

Looking back is universal for all of those impacted by suicide. For some, it is an attempt to formulate responses to the countless unanswered questions. For others, it is to gain some semblance of control over the situation. Regardless of the reason, life in rewind seems inevitable for the survivor. Unfortunately, for most of us, life in rewind rarely, if ever, yields the results we desire. In her book, *Night Falls Fast: Understanding Suicide*, Kay Redfield Jamison writes, "Each way to suicide is its own: intensely private, unknowable, and terrible. Suicide will have seemed to its perpetrator the last and best of bad possibilities, and any attempt by the living to chart this final terrain of life can be only a sketch, maddeningly incomplete."

Early on after my mom's suicide, I spent a few years ruminating the question of 'why?' Why did she kill herself? Why did she not tell anyone she was so depressed? Why did she not seek help? Why? Why? Why? My questions remained unanswered until I eventually stopped asking. Last year, though, twenty-four years after her suicide, a thought crossed my mind that finally answered those questions in a way that clicked for me: The 'why' will never make sense to someone who is free of mental illness. Even if our loved ones could come back and explain precisely why they took their own life, their reasoning would be insufficient to us. You see, there is absolutely no reason they could give us that would justify their death because, if we do not struggle with mental illness we can, quite possibly, never understand. We are not tormented by what they were tormented by nor do we feel the way they did. We cannot ever understand the depth of pain and emotional turmoil they were experiencing and, thus, can likely never comprehend why they felt death was their only option. Jamison continues :

It is tempting when looking at the life of anyone who has committed suicide to read into the decision to die a vastly complex web of reasons; and, of course, such complexity is warranted. No one illness or event causes suicide; and certainly no one knows all, or perhaps even most, of the motivations behind the killing of the self. But psychopathology is almost always there, and its deadliness is fierce. Love, success, and friendship are not always enough to counter the pain and destructiveness of severe mental illness.

Although I do not like the answer, it does give me some form of closure, or at the very least, allows me to stop asking 'why?'

I think, for many survivors, we believe closure can only come when we fully determine the cause of suicide. For some, as I mentioned above, it is a form of control. As humans, we love to believe we are in control. We believe that, if we can determine the cause of the suicide, we can then prevent another one in the future. Believing we can prevent suicide from happening again gives us the feeling of control in an otherwise very chaotic and unpredictable circumstance. There is nothing wrong in trying to determine the cause of suicide per se; the problem lies, however, in situations where the survivor gets stuck in this cycle. If a survivor is constantly ruminating over the cause and looking back and accepting blame for clues missed, then moving forward is impossible. When survivors get stuck, they are unable to grieve and accept the death. They are in grief-limbo, incapable of moving forward. When a person is fixated on a specific aspect of the death which will likely never be answered or changed, the grief will pause there, frozen, until the survivor is able to honestly evaluate it further. Suicide is not meant to be comprehended. Suicide does not make sense to those unaffected by mental illness.

As discussed in the guilt and shame chapter in this book, survivors often feel an intense level of guilt for not preventing the suicide. On one hand, it makes complete sense that we, as people who desperately loved this person, would feel some form of guilt for not preventing their death. If only they would have told me, I could have saved them. If only I knew they were depressed, I could have helped them get the help they needed. If only____ (fill in the blank). The truth, though, is, no, we could not have prevented it.

I hope you can hear this, accept it, and internalize it. We are not mind readers; we had no way of knowing our loved ones were contemplating suicide. In some circumstances, survivors may actually have been aware suicide was an option for their loved one. Still, we are not able to control other people's actions. For example, if I tell no one of my intention of killing myself and end my life right now, who is to blame?

Nobody! People cannot prevent that which they know nothing about, nor can they stop me from doing something I desperately want to do. I am my own person and get to make choices for myself. So were our loved ones. They were unique individuals whom we, sadly, could not control. They chose death to escape their pain, and we could do nothing to stop it. No amount of looking back at past conversations will change the results. I say this not to sound cold and heartless but instead to give you freedom from the burden of guilt and responsibility. I wish we could have done something to stop it, believe me. The reality, though, is we could not. Once we are able to remove the burden of guilt, we are then able to see their suicide for what is was: their escape from a pain we may never fully know or comprehend.

LaRita Archibald wrote a piece titled "Reinforcement in the Aftermath of Suicide." When I read this piece, it put suicide in perspective for me. It allowed me to see my mom's pain and recognize her choice to die was her own. I neither caused it nor could I have prevented it. This gave me freedom to say my mom was her own individual, and I cannot take responsibility in any capacity for her death. I am including the entire written piece below because it is incredibly powerful and freeing. Every survivor should have the opportunity to experience and internalize these words.

REINFORCEMENT IN THE AFTERMATH OF SUICIDE
LaRita Archibald

RESPONSIBILITY: Putting it into perspective.

I have a responsibility <u>TO</u> those I love...

> to be loving, patient, considerate and kind,
> to be loyal, respectful and honest,
> to be appreciative, encouraging and comforting,
> to share myself and care for myself;
> .....to be the best possible "ME".......

BUT

I am not responsible <u>FOR</u> them...

> not for their achievements, successes or triumphs,
> not for their joy, gratification or fulfillment,
> not for their defeats, failures or disappointments,
> not for their thoughts, choices or mistakes,
> .....And, most of all, not for their suicide.......

For <u>HAD</u> I been responsible, this death would not have occurred.

***

To assume responsibility for this death, or to place responsibility upon another, robs the one who died of their personhood and invalidates the enormity of their pain and their desperate need for relief.

***

THE PROCESS DEFINED:

ANGER is my protest against my loss and its cause. Anger is an effort to control that which cannot be controlled or changed.

ANGER is energy that cannot be denied, destroyed or forgotten; but energy that must be expressed lest it become a pool of hatred, resentment and bitterness within myself, depriving me of well-being, dignity, peace of mind, wholesome relationships and my hope for future happiness...and so,

it must be converted

into

UNDERSTANDING this death resulted from another's distorted "grief"; from viewing their life situation and their ability to exist within it, with doubt, fear and hopelessness and not as it, in fact, existed.

ACCEPTANCE this death and its cause cannot be changed;

this loss is part of my life;

this part is not the whole of my life.

RECONCILIATION my life is forever changed by this death, but it is not destroyed

I CAN and WILL live through and beyond this loss.

I WILL NOT always hurt as badly as I do today

I WILL have happiness and peace of mind in my life again

through

FORGIVENESS is allowing myself and others the humanness to have made mistakes, even of this magnitude. I don't have to like it!

is relinquishing anger, guilt and the need to fault and blame.

does not mean finding reasons, causes or justification for my loved one's death.

does not mean forgetting. I will never forget!

does not mean being completely free of emotional pain, but allowing anguish and despair to transition into sorrow and regret

achieving

RESURRECTION **living again**…free of emotional bondage to the fact of suicide; free of emotional bondage to the one who died.

and

taking back into myself, as sustaining strength, treasured memory of the life shared with my loved one.

©LRA 1985

Questions to Consider

How does it feel to recognize we may never know the reason someone took their life and, if we did, we may never fully understand it?

Have you experienced living your life in rewind? Do you find yourself constantly looking back in order to look for clues missed?

Do you place blame on yourself, believing you could have done more to prevent it?

Was there a specific truth you were able to pull from the piece shared at the end of this chapter, "Reinforcement in the Aftermath of Suicide"?

CHAPTER 8

Forgiveness

"Forgiveness is not always easy. At times, it feels more painful than the wound we suffered, to forgive the one that inflicted it. And yet, there is no peace without forgiveness. Attack thoughts towards others are attack thoughts towards ourselves. The first step in forgiveness is the willingness to forgive."

—Marianne Williamson

Forgiveness, on the surface, seems easy and straightforward, but, in reality, it is quite the opposite. Forgiveness has many facets and is never truly complete. I like to look at life most of the time in black and white, but forgiveness forces me to explore the grey. This chapter explores the complexity of forgiveness: what it is exactly, what it is not, how to forgive, why we ought to, and the benefits of doing so.

After my mom's suicide, I was incredibly hurt and felt betrayed, rejected, and abandoned. Instead of openly exploring those emotions, I chose to stuff them instead and cover them with anger. It was easier, for me, to simply be angry with my mom forever for what I deemed an incredibly selfish act. I realize not all survivors deal with the level of anger I did, nor do they carry as much resentment, but that is how I responded. About fifteen years after her suicide and with three years of weekly therapy, I began to see the toll anger and a lack of forgiveness was having on me. There is a popular quote by an unknown source that says, "Unforgiveness is like drinking poison yourself and waiting for the other person to die." Most of my life I believed if I forgave my mom, I would somehow be letting her off the hook or even condoning her actions. The reality is I was drinking the deadly poison and waiting for my mom to die. My anger and lack of forgiveness wasn't hurting my mom in any capacity; she was already dead. My lack of forgiveness, instead, was only hurting me. Thus began my journey of forgiveness.

What Forgiveness Is Not

In his book, *Total Forgiveness*, R.T. Kendall discusses ten things forgiveness is not:

Approval of what they did
Excusing what they did
Justifying what they did
Pardoning what they did
Reconciliation
Denying what they did
Blindness to what happened
Forgetting
Refusing to take the wrong seriously
Pretending we are not hurt

For me, the hardest part of forgiving my mom for choosing to die was feeling like I was letting her off the hook for doing something so painful to me. Kendall speaks to this specifically, "Some people may think that in order to forgive they must dismiss a wrong or pass it off as inconsequential or insignificant. But that is only avoiding the problem, possibly trying to make forgiveness easier. The greater victory for the one who does the forgiving is to face up to the seriousness-even the wickedness- of what happened and still forgive."

According to the list above, forgiveness is not about forgetting what they have done or lessening the impact. In fact, it says quite the opposite. Forgiveness is recognizing the pain, acknowledging the hurt caused, and consciously choosing to move forward.

What Forgiveness Is:

Merriam-Webster defines 'forgive' as follows: "To cease to feel resentment against (an offender)." It does not say forgiveness forces me to like or excuse what she did. Instead, forgiveness is simply choosing to stop feeling anger and resentment toward her. That's it. Forgiveness is much more for us than it is the person we are forgiving. Our loved ones do not require our forgiveness. They are no longer here. Our hearts and minds, though, are very much in need of forgiving and letting go.

Why We Ought to Forgive

Research has proven that refusing to forgive others can take a toll on our bodies as well as our mental health. Here are just a few symptoms that can develop if one is unable to forgive.

Physical: Inability to sleep, weakened immune system, an outward body appearance that begins to manifest the internal misery, relationship struggles, aches and pains, and even illness or disease.

Mental/Emotional: stress, anger, resentment, anxiety, depression, and the inability to move forward.

In 2006 I decided I needed to finally forgive my mom. I made a big deal out of it, rented a room on the beach alone, and wrote on a balloon all the things I was forgiving her for: leaving me, causing me to find her body, forcing me to grow up without my mom, etc. Once I had written everything, I said a quick prayer and released the balloon into the sky. It was, in that moment, very freeing as I saw all I had been holding inside for fifteen years float away. The burden on my heart and shoulders seemed to fly away as well. I figured since I finally forgave her I would be all set and ready to take on the world with my newfound freedom!

Unfortunately, that was not the case. As I discussed in "The Path of Grief" chapter, life events seem to trigger a lot in our hearts and minds. Forgiveness often requires us to forgive repeatedly. Sometimes we even need to forgive daily. I liken this to peeling an onion. Each layer peeled brings about different and, sometimes, new reasons to forgive. New layers can still bring tears and new emotions, but that in no way negates the prior act of forgiveness. Sometimes people feel they are not truly forgiving if they need to repeatedly forgive. This is simply not true. Before I was ever married I did not need to forgive my mom for missing my wedding because it had not yet taken place. When my wedding actually occurred, however, I did need to forgive her. Did my need to forgive her for missing my wedding signal that my releasing of the balloon on the beach years before was not a genuine act? No. It just meant that a new life events triggered the need to forgive again. Whenever we feel hurt, sad, angry, abandoned, rejected, or any other emotion linked to the suicide of our loved one, we may need to forgive again. And again. And again. It is an ongoing process as we navigate life.

In a powerful blog titled, "But So AM I," written by Darnell Young for *The Gift of Second*, Darnell shares her thoughts on her mom's suicide:

> I used to think suicide was so selfish. I still do, to be honest. But so am I. On my best, happiest, most clear-headed days, I am selfish. In little ways and big ways... intentional and unintentional... I make decisions every day that are all about me. I'm not proud of that, but I know there is grace for me in those moments. So when I am selfish even on a great day, I cannot possibly expect someone to be selfless on the darkest, most desperate day of their life. I cannot be angry that in a very confused and lonely state, she was imperfect. I must have grace for that. And I've found that allowing her to be imperfect and selfish during such a vulnerable time has

given me a lot of freedom, and it has kept anger from robbing me of my joy.

Darnell's perspective on her mother's worst and last day is one that allows forgiveness to naturally enter in. I wish I had read these words twenty-five years ago, as it would have saved me a lot of anger and allowed me more freedom and joy.

How to Forgive

We know our loved ones are no longer here, and we are unable to have a face to face conversation. So, how do we forgive someone who is no longer alive? Any way we want! It's easy, really. Remember, we are not forgiving them for their sake; we are forgiving them for our own. It does not matter how you actually go about it; rather, the important part is simply the act of forgiving. You can pretend they are in the room with you and have a verbal monologue as you tell your loved one you are forgiving them. You can write out all of the things you are specifically forgiving them for in journal form. You can release a balloon like I did. You can verbally forgive them as you spread their ashes at a favorite destination. You can write it on a rock and then throw it in the ocean. You can do whatever is meaningful and healing to you. There is no wrong way to forgive your loved one. If you wake up tomorrow and feel angry again, it's okay. You do not need to make it an elaborate production each time you forgive. A simple, "I forgive you today for not being here on my birthday," is sufficient and you can move on.

The act of forgiveness can be freeing. In the examples mentioned above, many involve throwing, releasing, or writing something, and this is intentional. When we harbor unforgiveness, we stuff it inside and allow it to grow and fester, but when we physically release something, it allows for it to leave our bodies, and we feel both the physical and emotional release of that burden. A tangible display of forgiveness can be powerful!

Are You in Need of Forgiving Yourself?

Survivors often share they feel no need to forgive their loved one because they understand they struggled with mental illness and just wanted the pain to end. Sometimes, though, survivors are in need of forgiving themselves. Many survivors struggle with the guilt of not doing enough to prevent the suicide or save their loved one. The survivor carries the guilt, sometimes, for the rest of their life. This is also a time we need to forgive. In this case, though, we are forgiving ourselves. R.T. Kendall wrote, "The ability to forgive ourselves comes partly from understanding guilt. Guilt is, at heart, a feeling that one is to blame. For example, when you blame others, you have kept a record of their wrongs. But when you blame yourself, you have kept a record of your own wrongs."

No matter how much you feel the need to blame yourself for the suicide of your loved one, you cannot take responsibility. If we could have prevented it, we would have. Kendall goes on to write, "Forgiving yourself may bring about the breakthrough you have been looking for. It could set you free in ways you have never before experienced."

If you have felt stuck and have already forgiven your loved one, you may want to explore the need to forgive yourself for any blame or guilt you carry today. Perhaps saying to yourself, "You are not to blame for this death. You loved them and tried to help in every way. Their choice to die does not reflect your inability to love or protect. Their choice to die was their decision to end their own pain. It had nothing to do with you and you could not have prevented it. It is okay to forgive yourself."

Forgiving ourselves can look a lot like the tangible expressions of forgiveness listed above or it can simply be the awareness of self-blame. Once we discover thoughts of self-blame creeping into our minds, we can choose to replace those thoughts with more accurate positive self-talk. We gain nothing from continually blaming ourselves for someone else's suicide, but we have everything to gain by forgiving ourselves. When you notice yourself taking blame for the suicide, you can mentally tell yourself, "I did not cause this. I wanted them to stay but they chose to leave. I loved them and would have done anything to prevent this. I cannot take ownership for their decision."

Forgiveness, in the end, brings about freedom like nothing else can. When we are willing to forgive others and ourselves, we remove burdens we were never meant to carry. Forgiveness frees us to move forward in our grieving process and allows us to heal. Forgiveness is difficult but oh so necessary to our own well-being. In the words of Maya Angelou, "It's one of the greatest gifts you can give yourself, to forgive. Forgive everybody." I would add, "and forgive yourself."

Questions to Consider
Do you think forgiveness is necessary? Why or why not?
Have you seen areas in your own life (physical or mental) that have been negatively affected due to not forgiving? Explain.
What do you think about unforgiveness being similar to drinking poison?
What do you think about the list explaining all the things forgiveness is not? Does this change your perception of forgiveness at all?
Have you forgiven your loved one for choosing suicide?
Are there some areas in which you may need to consider forgiving yourself?
What is the payoff for not forgiving either them or yourself?

CHAPTER 9

How a Specific Loss Affects How We Grieve

"I wonder if my first breath was as soul-stirring to my mother as her last breath was to me."

—LISA GOICH

SUICIDE IS DEVASTATING for those left behind regardless of their relationship to the deceased. The guilt, shock, and grief are universal and even overwhelming at times. After talking with and interviewing countless survivors for *The Gift of Second*, I began to notice some common beliefs, emotions, feelings, and experiences within specific loss groups. I created subgroups (parents, children, spouses, siblings, and friends) and then began surveying folks in order to get a better understanding for the commonalities within these subgroups. I share this research with you now in hopes of normalizing your own feelings and also allowing you to hear from fellow survivors who have expressed similar experiences.

Of course all the information shared below is not absolute, but these are the most common responses received, and I hope you will be able to find common ground with others and recognize, again, that you are not alone.

To Those Who Lost a Child

The resounding emotion for parents who have lost a child is the intense and profound feeling of guilt. Parents expressed this sentiment more than all other survivors in all of the other subgroups combined. Parents articulated time and time again the guilt for not being able to save their own child. Each parent surveyed explained they feel guilt for not seeing their child's pain and the impending suicide, not being able to save their child, and not doing more to get their child the help they needed. Several parents interviewed also expressed a level of second-guessing themselves in the way they parented. "Was I too hard on him? Where did I fail as a parent that my own child could not come talk to me about how he/she was feeling? Did I fail to convey how much I loved them?"

Most parents also shared the common fear for the safety of the remaining living children. "Will they also kill themselves?" is a common question which parents find themselves ruminating. The fear of a repeat suicide within the home caused parents a tremendous amount of anxiety and pain. Some parents, however, used this fear to become more protective of their children and also more involved in their lives. They became more proactive in talking with their children as they were, this time, more in tune with the symptoms of depression and the benefits of open dialogue.

Parents also expressed the difficulty in knowing how to talk about their son or daughter as life continues. They explained the pain they experience each time a new person asks them if they have children and how many. Parents dread these questions as they do not know how to respond or what to say to questions such as, "How old are your kids and what do they do for a living?" Moms and dads both explained they don't want to exclude their deceased child from the conversation, but the difficulty in having to explain they are no longer alive and the cause of death is troubling.

I asked each survivor if they had wisdom or advice to share with other survivors within their specific subgroup, and the following is for other parents who have lost a child.

"You are not alone. You did nothing wrong. It is not your fault. It is horrible. It sucks. There are days you don't know how you will live on, but you do. You have to. Take your experience and use it to educate and raise awareness. One day at a time. It's okay not to be okay."

"Keep moving forward; keep talking about it. Don't let the way they died be a secret. Keep your face toward hope. If we keep talking about it openly we can help save others."

"This is the hardest thing you will ever deal with in your life. Nothing hurts and breaks you like losing a child, especially to suicide. Don't let anyone tell you when to do things or tell you how you should feel."

"Grief counseling is very important. You never get over it; you work your way through it. It helps to talk with others who have suffered a similar bereavement, as others (who have not) don't understand how we feel."

Losing a Parent

This subgroup had several common themes dependent on the age of the child at the time of their parent's suicide. All participants in this study were adults at the time of the interview, but the age of the individual at the time of their parent's suicide varies greatly. Small children, for example, expressed an intense development of anxiety and fear. They conveyed that after their parent died, they constantly feared the other parent would also die, leaving them to become an orphan. The type of death they feared in the surviving parent was irrelevant, but rather their fear of being without parents was the greatest stressor. Several expressed a continuing struggle with anxiety into adulthood as well.

A similar belief in several children, regardless of age at the time of their parent's death, is the feeling of not being valued enough that their parent wanted to stay alive. Several children expressed not feeling lovable, worthy, valuable, or enough in the eyes of their parents. Almost all of the participants expressed an inability to trust others, explaining, "If my own parent could abandon me like this, how can I ever trust others to stick around?" These doubts of self-worth and the inability to trust others have, often, continued throughout life.

Children also expressed intense levels of anger toward their parent for abandoning them. Some children, who were adults themselves at the time of their parent's suicide, expressed great sadness for their parent missing out on major milestones in the child's life such as getting married, having kids (the first would-be grandchildren), and job placements.

Some wisdom from others who have lost a parent to suicide:

"The pain does eventually become less intense. I would encourage you to seek out a support group for survivors of suicide loss. Connecting with others who "get it" can be just the help you need."
"Write them a letter or do some journaling and tell them that you love them and in time you will forgive them for leaving you."
"Their decision to die was not because they didn't love you or because you were not worth living for. Their decision to die was out of their own hopelessness."
"Let yourself be angry and not okay. Let yourself feel all of it. Focus on all the good memories but also accept the bad ones, too. Work on it. It's going to be a long journey, but don't do it alone. The worst thing you could do is not talk about it."

Losing a Spouse/Partner

Many spouses expressed intense grief at the loss of their future together with their spouse. Several survivors conveyed a deep sadness and could remember feeling an overwhelming desire to join their partner in death in the aftermath of the suicide because the grief was simply too much. Each survivor expressed feeling lonely. One woman shared, "It's a couple's world. I never noticed it before. It's really lonely to, all of a sudden, be single."

This subgroup explained the unique struggle of trying to help their children through their grief while grieving themselves and not wanting to show too much pain and emotion for fear of scaring their children. These parents also explained that one of the only things that got them through the pain and devastation initially was the responsibility of continuing to care for the children in their home.

Anger was a common theme within this subgroup, but the cause of anger varied. Some were angry at their spouse for leaving them to raise children alone and angry their spouse caused so much pain to their offspring. Many were angry about the financial burden they now carried alone. A sentiment that was repeated endlessly was anger about both being single again and anger toward friends and family for trying to set the survivor up on dates because "it was time to start dating again." One survivor remembered feeling, "I don't want to go on a date with another person--all I want is my husband back!"

Many spouses expressed feeling betrayed because they had no idea the depth of pain their spouse was experiencing or they discovered a 'hidden life' their spouse was living (such as an addiction or debt) that the survivor can never get answers to, causing the survivor to question how much of their relationship was real.

Some wisdom from other spouses:

"You're going to be okay. It doesn't feel like it right now but you are going to be okay."
"I have been angry at what my wife did to me and our children. I have found that talking with other survivors of suicide loss has been the most helpful."
"Our loved ones were thinking with a broken brain that was more powerful than their heart, which was still full of love for us."
"It's okay to date again. You don't have to feel guilty about it. It's also okay to not date again. You don't need to feel pressured into it."

Losing a Sibling

Many of those who have lost a sibling explained they feel overlooked and minimalized. They conveyed that their parents received a lot of emotional support as did the spouse and children of the sibling, but the surviving sibling received minimal attention and care. Many expressed feeling as if their loss was discounted by friends and even family members.

Guilt is a recurring theme within this subgroup as well. Several siblings conveyed being best friends with their sibling and feeling guilty for not doing more to help them or even recognizing the amount of pain they were experiencing. One sibling expressed guilt for not helping her brother more and instead "waited on the sidelines for something to change" while another sibling expressed feeling guilt because "we failed to prove how much we loved him." Overwhelming anxiety is commonly shared within this subgroup as well. "I suddenly feel like life is fragile and anyone could die at any moment." Anger and grief were commonly expressed with one person sharing, "I feel grief for happy childhood memories that are now tainted."

Several siblings expressed that the suicide strengthened their relationships with their parents, and they could now talk openly with them about their sibling, while others conveyed the overwhelming stress and responsibility of having to care for the grieving parents that seemed unable to move forward. One survivor wrote, "I'm now an only child and provide the emotional support to my grieving parents who can't seek external support on their own."

Some, not all, siblings have felt the pressure, whether consciously or sub-consciously and whether expected or not, to fill in the gap of their now absent sibling. Whether it is personality traits like humor, interests, or being readily available to other family members, one sibling expressed, "I feel the pressure to be smarter, healthier, and funnier. I'm always trying to be like my brother to keep my dad happy."

Some wisdom from other siblings:

"Don't let your sibling's life choice affect you to the point where you can't live your own life."

"I am not sure there is a right set of words. I would hug you, tell you I understand and let you cry or talk or be quiet or whatever you need to do. I would just be with you."

"No two people grieve the same way. Your relationship with that person was your own, and therefore your grieving might be different than others."

"Don't blame yourself and be kind to yourself."

A Friend

The overwhelming feelings for friends are feeling alone, isolated, and discounted. Several friends expressed feeling left out and forced to grieve alone because they were not family. One friend shared she wanted to be more involved in planning her best friend's memorial service as a way to honor her, but the family refused to allow her to help. Some friends explained the difficulty in not being known by the surviving family because they lived in separate cities or states but had been extremely close to the one who died. As a result, the surviving friend was treated as a stranger by the family despite her close relationship to her friend. Others explained if there were not mutual friends to grieve with, the surviving friend was isolated in their own pain.

Guilt, again, is a common feeling within this subgroup, as these friends shared everything with one another and to not know the enormity of depression and agony their friend felt is devastating. Frustration that their friend did not speak of their pain is common. Some expressed anger and confusion, as they had made plans with their friend in the coming days and then killed themselves without any clue. They conveyed sadness that the one who died left a note to the family only without any mention of the friend.

One survivor expressed not feeling like he fit in at a grief group he attended because he was 'just' a friend and felt other members in the group discounted his grief as minimal because he did not lose a family member. The themes for this subgroup were alone and lonely. These were mentioned time and time again.

Some wisdom from friends:

"Be gracious with yourself and take care of yourself. Don't expect things to make sense. Don't expect forgiveness to come easily. Don't expect to have it all figured out. It doesn't make sense. It may take a really long time but be kind to yourself."

"Don't let their death shake your love for them. It's okay to be mad and hurt, but when those feeling are gone you will realize that you still love them and miss them."

"Attend a bereavement group specific to friends such as *Friends in Grief*."

The responses from these subgroups clearly illustrated the fact that each person's relationship with the one who died is unique in the same way the impact of each loss is unique. In *Modern Man in Search of a Soul*, Carl Jung wrote, "The shoe that fits one person pinches another; there is no recipe for living that suits all cases." I think the same can be true for grieving, and yet there is something freeing and valuable in knowing others who have suffered the same type of loss fully understand the depth of pain. In these subgroups we realize we are really never alone.

Questions to Consider

Have you felt, even among other survivors, that nobody understands your pain specifically?

Do you feel you are able to relate to others within your same subgroup?

What is it like to know there are others who have experienced the same emotions and thoughts you have?

Is there anything else you would include that was not listed in your sub-group?

What do you wish others could know about the specific pain you carry?

CHAPTER 10

The First Year

"Without you in my arms, I feel an emptiness in my soul. I find myself searching the crowds for your face- I know it's an impossibility, but I cannot help myself."

— NICHOLAS SPARKS, *MESSAGE IN A BOTTLE*

THE FIRST YEAR after a suicide often feels chaotic, overwhelming, and confusing. As we try to navigate life without our loved one, we are also faced with the difficult task of handling the logistics after a death. Not only is our grief painful and debilitating, but we are also forced to make choices that are, often, beyond our capacity in our current state of mind.

The first week we can feel numb. We are in shock, yet trying to get word out to all friends and family and planning and attending the funeral. Usually, though, this first week is full of people. Friends and family gather from all over and mourn together as they sit in disbelief of the death of our loved one. Many survivors, however, have expressed they felt completely alone after the funeral. When our loved ones who were so helpful and caring during that first week return home and back to their normal lives, we can feel lost and helpless.

We face the difficult tasks of cleaning out our loved one's home and determining what to do with all of his possessions while also trying to figure out financial matters such as life insurance, bank accounts, and real estate. These tasks are confusing and overwhelming for anyone, but when we add the trauma, shock, and grief of a suicide, these matters can sometimes be too much. Many survivors find it too daunting to even begin, so they choose to do nothing instead. Houses where our loved one lived can remain empty and untouched for months or even years because the thought of going through all their possessions seems both too painful and final. Countless survivors have mentioned never touching their loved one's bedroom, car, or personal space such as a garage or office again because to do so would make their death real and permanent.

To navigate logistics after the loss of a loved one is painful and taxing to say the least. These situations may be the perfect time to call a friend or family member to step in and help. Often our loved ones want to help but they have no idea how to, and so they stay away. This would be a great time for you to reach out to someone you trust and ask for help. Maybe you need to hire a financial advisor or real estate agent to handle the technical aspects and confusing contracts. It can be helpful to have a friend assist with sorting through your loved one's belongings. Some of these tasks have time sensitive deadlines. Some have accumulating bills such as ongoing rent/mortgage payments, while others can be postponed a bit. Regardless of the task, it is okay to ask for help. The best person to choose is someone you trust and someone who will be sensitive to what you need and want while honoring both you and your loved ones. Avoid asking anyone to help you if you sense they will be draining or add any drama. This person should be there simply to provide support to you.

Big Decisions on Hold

It has been widely accepted never to make big decisions in life for the first year following the death of a loved one. This is important advice to consider. Sometimes decisions must be made due to financial reasons, like selling a home or liquidating assets to pay off bills or expenses. Sometimes it is necessary and unpreventable. Other decisions, though, such as moving homes, switching jobs, getting married, having a baby, or making other life altering and possibly permanent decisions are best to wait on. Sometimes, in our mourning, we have thoughts or ideas that we may later regret when we are not so consumed by grief.

The suggestion that no big decisions be made for the first six to twelve months is so that you can avoid regretting a hasty decision later or avoid getting yourself into a situation you cannot get out of. Many survivors revealed they sold their home and moved to a new house because they couldn't imagine living in their home any longer without their loved one. Then, down the road, they came to regret the choice to hastily move; they would love to have remained in the home where so many memories were made. (Of course, this may not be the case if your loved one died in that home and you are moving away from the constant reminder of the trauma, as I did).

Another big decision to avoid is getting involved in a romantic relationship too early. It is difficult to grieve in the first place, but to add a new relationship that involves emotional investment is almost impossible in light of the pain you are still sifting through. Although none of these rules are absolutes, the best policy during the first year is to practice self-care and allow yourself the least amount of change by reducing the need to make life-altering decisions.

Year of Firsts

One of the most difficult aspects of the first year is what is often referred to as the Year of Firsts. The Year of Firsts is all of the first times we experience an event, holiday, or tradition without our loved one. This includes birthdays, holidays, vacations, events, seasons, or any other life event we are now navigating without them.

Survivors often talk about the difficulty of the first Thanksgiving or Christmas after the suicide and how to handle the typical traditions and expectations from others. Oftentimes, we have traditions we have always participated in, whether it be decorating in a certain manner, cutting down our own Christmas tree, or hosting a celebration. Maybe these were our loved one's ideas originally, or maybe they simply loved participating in them. Whatever the case may be, it can sometimes produce dread as the season approaches.

This is a good time to evaluate if you want to continue with the traditions. You might need to look at them this year and ask yourself, "Do I really want to continue with these?" You might think, "We have to do it because my loved one adored participating in it" or "We always do that tradition. We can't skip it this year." This might be a good time, though, to look at those traditions and honestly assess if you have the desire, energy, and ability to continue with them. If you decide you do not, then it is important to give yourself permission to skip them.

This might also be a great time to create new traditions. These do not have to be permanent, they may only be temporary for the first year or two. I remember always celebrating Christmas Eve with my mom's side of the family, but after she died, my dad, brother, and I decided it would be too painful to attend the celebration. We decided to go out to a nice dinner and then a movie together instead. We did this for only the first two years, but it was what we needed during such a difficult time that would have otherwise been a constant reminder of my mom's absence. It did not make the season pain free; instead, it simply gave us an opportunity to choose how we wanted to spend those difficult days and lessen the pain just a bit.

The Year of Firsts might also involve how to navigate annual vacations or trips that have always been a family favorite. It is okay to continue with this trip if it is something you feel would be enjoyable and will find pleasure in. If, however, it is something you are dreading, it is okay to cancel the trip or perhaps change the destination. The important thing to remember during the Year of Firsts is that it is okay to say no to celebrations and change or cancel plans entirely. You need to do what you are comfortable with and what you can manage emotionally and physically. We don't want to just endure events for the sake of keeping with tradition. We want to take care of ourselves the best way possible (see the chapter on self-care).

Often, society tells us we should be done mourning by the first anniversary of our loved one's death. Sometimes we believe this ourselves. The truth is it is not realistic to expect our grieving to be complete and wrapped up nicely simply because we turned the twelfth page on the calendar. We do a disservice to ourselves when we believe everything will be easier once we make it through the first year and then later beat ourselves up when we recognize life is still hard. It is important to note the anniversary is merely one day; it is not the culmination of grief. As I explained in the grief cycle chapter, there is no absolute timeline when we can expect to be 'over' this incredible loss. To expect the first year anniversary to be the magic day when mourning and pain disappears is unfair to ourselves.

Unfortunately, many survivors share their second year was actually harder than the first. I mention this not to be discouraging but to give you insight instead. I remember walking around in a constant state of shock the entire first year and then slowly recognizing the finality of her death. It was then, in the second year, that life became less about 'firsts' and more about the new reality of life without my mom. Also, I think people expect us to have moved on by the completion of the first year and, thus, they stop asking us how we are doing, stop seeing how they can help, and stop thinking about our pain. It felt a bit lonelier beginning that second year. This is not to scare you but rather to normalize it so you do not have false expectations but a more realistic understanding instead. This is normal to experience.

Moving on with Life

In addition to everything mentioned above, it is important to discuss feelings of guilt survivors often experience regarding moving on with life. Sometimes we feel guilty for laughing and finding joy again or for changing traditions or dating a new partner. All of these are normal life events for those still living, yet survivors can feel a tremendous amount of guilt for continuing on with life. It is important, yet again, to give yourself permission to live life and seek joy and happiness. Your loved one would not want you to be miserable, depressed, and to stop living your own life. You are still alive and have a beautiful life ahead of you if you can embrace it. Do not feel guilty for wanting to find happiness. Life goes on.

Tessa Shaffer, author of *Heaven Has No Regrets*, wrote the following:

Death will paint everything a different shade of remorse.

You'll feel guilty that you're still breathing.
    But you can't stop.
You'll feel guilty for wanting to laugh again.
    And it will be awful the first time that you do.
You'll feel guilty for just about everything at first.
And someday, at some point, you'll start to feel guilty . . .
    for forgetting to feel guilty.

But of all Heaven's lessons, guilt isn't one of them. You don't need to hold on to it. It doesn't need to be a practice and it shouldn't be your life.

    Heaven would never approve of your guilt.
    Because Heaven has no regrets.

The first year is one full of shock, pain, trauma, and lots and lots of tears. Be kind to yourself. Don't expect too much from yourself. There is a popular expression which says, "Grief is a marathon, not a sprint." I think that applies, especially, to the first year. It is completely normal if things that were once easy for you such as work or projects become challenging. Grief can impact so many areas of your life, including your own physical health. Be compassionate with yourself and these temporary limitations. It won't always be this difficult. And, be gracious with yourself when life is still really hard beyond the first year or tasks remain challenging for a while. It is a journey. John Irving, author of, *A Prayer for Owen Meany*, paints well the first year for a survivor:

When someone you love dies, and you're not expecting it, you don't lose her all at once; you lose her in pieces over a long time- the way the mail stops coming, and her scent fades from the pillows and even from the clothes in her closet and drawers. Gradually, you accumulate the parts of her that are gone. Just when the day comes—when there's a particular missing part that overwhelms you with the feeling that she's gone, forever—there comes another day, and another specifically missing part.

Be kind to yourself. The grief of a suicide loss will be exhausting, confusing, painful, and often debilitating. Ask for help, take things slow, and try to avoid any unnecessary big decisions. Set realistic expectations for yourself and give yourself permission to take life one day at a time.

Questions to Consider

What has been the hardest part of the Year of Firsts for you?

Have you felt comfortable asking people for help when you need it? If not, what is preventing you from doing so?

Have you avoided cleaning out homes or bedrooms of your loved one? Does it feel too final/permanent to do so?

Did you believe your grief would be final by the completion of the first year?

What do you think of the idea of putting big decisions on hold for a while?

CHAPTER 11

Self-Care

"Caring for myself is not self-indulgence, it is self-preservation..."

—AUDRE LORDE

AFTER THE LOSS of a loved one we are, typically, in so much shock and devastation that we do not even know how to continue on in life let alone take care of ourselves. Sometimes we have children or other family members who need our care and attention, and so we focus on them at the sacrifice of ourselves. Other times we believe we can continue on in life, living as we were before the suicide. Maybe we discount the impact of the trauma and believe we *should* move on by now. Whatever the case may be, self-care is often overlooked, pushed aside, or believed to be unimportant. Unfortunately, when we do not take care of ourselves, everyone pays the price.

When we get on an airplane and the flight attendants run through the safety procedures, they always explain when the oxygen masks fall from the ceiling, "It is crucial to first put your own on before assisting your children or the person sitting next to you." They say this because if we spend all of our time and energy helping someone else, neglecting our own need for oxygen, we will pass out and be of no assistance to anyone. Instead, if we first take care of ourselves, we are then able to care for anyone around us who is struggling. The same is true when it comes to self-care.

Sometimes we believe taking care of ourselves is selfish and we would be better off helping others who need us instead. This could not be more inaccurate. Why do firefighters take the time to put on oxygen masks and protective uniforms before rescuing others trapped in a fire? It's simple, really. They would not be able to save anyone if they did not first protect and care for themselves when fighting the dangerous flames. The same is true for us. After a trauma and devastating loss like suicide, it is imperative to take care of ourselves. People often feel self-care is selfish and unnecessary. The next time that thought comes into your mind, think of the firefighter rushing into a burning building with no uniform, mask, or oxygen. Think about how far he will get into the building before needing to run outside for fresh air.

We are of no help to others if we refuse to take care of ourselves first. What is self-care exactly? Self-care is simply making conscious choices to take care of your mental, emotional, and physical health. It will look different for everyone. Let's look at some different ways self-care can be implemented and how it can benefit each of us.

It's Okay to Say "No."

We often feel we need to commit to all things and all people because, if we don't, we will feel rude or unsupportive. Sometimes we say yes to things because people 'expect' us to. The truth is nobody can say yes all the time, and we need to be okay with it. Sometimes the best way we can take care of ourselves is by saying no to commitments, obligations, and responsibilities. If a friend or family member invites you over to their home for a holiday because you always spend that holiday with them but it feels overwhelming this year to even think about going, much less prepare the feast you typically do, it is okay to say, "I'm not feeling up to it this year. I think I will stay home instead." If you typically run the PTA at your child's school but the responsibility is too much to bear, it is okay to step down for a season (or permanently). If you and your friends always go on a huge summer vacation with all of your families and pets and this year it seems like too much to even consider, it is okay to say no. Sometimes the best self-care we can possibly do is to say no and lighten our loads. In the aftermath of a suicide, we typically need less on our plates, not more. If we fill every minute of every day, avoidance, not grieving, is actually taking place. Self-care involves grieving and giving ourselves what we need during the grieving process. People will not always understand or agree with you saying "no" and that is okay. It is called 'self-care' not 'care for everyone else first.'

For a season it is perfectly fine to say no to people, things, and commitments. If, however, you are saying no all of the time and find yourself completely isolated and removed from friends and family, it is likely depression instead of self-care. At that point, it is necessary to talk with your doctor. Self-care is intended to promote better health and is a preventative step to feeling overwhelmed. If you are simply removing yourself from the world, you may need to evaluate a deeper cause.

Exercise

Exercise is one of the best things you can do for yourself. Exercise allows the body to release endorphins and gives the body the opportunity to feel positive again. Exercise does not need to be an hour of heavy cardio, weight-training, and push-ups. It can be if you want it to, but for most of us, exercise may be a 20- to 30-minute walk around our neighborhood, swimming some laps in the pool, or riding our bike around the park. The type of exercise does not matter; what *is* important is to get the body moving and those endorphins released.

Scheduling Time with People

An enjoyable way to practice self-care is to surround ourselves with people we love. If there is a friend you enjoy being with that fills you up instead of leaving you drained, then schedule time to see them regularly. Regular time together, whether weekly or monthly, is an important part of self-care. This is a time when you can be yourself, check-in with one another, and laugh together. This is a time to enjoy one another, catch a movie, grab lunch, play golf, etc.— a time to simply be with people you love doing things you enjoy. The most important aspect though is to schedule this time together. Simply saying, "we should get together soon" rarely results in time spent together at all. Instead, be intentional about picking a date that works, writing it in your calendar, and committing to making it happen. This is such a necessary component of self-care.

Finding a Hobby or Activity

On the surface, this one can often feel like more work. It's not though: it is actually something that can breathe life into you instead. The purpose of this is to provide an outlet you enjoy and the opportunity to lose yourself in it temporarily. For some people this is running, making music, painting, quilting, golfing, fishing, or writing. I have heard from several survivors that after their loved one's suicide, they picked up a new hobby, and it became a time for them to process through the suicide in a creative or positive manner that simply dialoguing about would not allow. One man told me he signed up for his first half-marathon and spent months training. It was in those early morning runs he could think, yell, cry, and process through his dad's suicide all alone while working toward a goal. Another survivor told me she always enjoyed art, but after her dad's suicide, she enrolled in an art class and used this new talent as a way to express her grief. Pick something that you are interested in that allows you to be creative, or set a goal and just keep showing up. You don't have to be good at it right now, you just have to want to participate in it. The rest will fall into place.

Traps To Be Aware Of

If we are not consciously taking care of ourselves, something or someone will fill that void for us. This is a dangerous place to be. In his book, *What to Do When the Police Leave: A Guide to the First Days of Traumatic Loss*, Bill Jenkins writes, "It is very easy to see the allure of alcohol to dull the pain and the temptation to punish myself for something that is not my fault. But the sobering truth is that if I step onto the path of self-destruction, I know I will never come back. "

Sometimes we do not want to consciously take care of ourselves. Sometimes we would rather numb the pain and pretend the suicide never happened and act like we are okay. The truth is, we are not okay. How could we be? Someone we desperately loved chose to end their life. How on earth could we be okay? French playwright Molière once stated, "If you suppress grief too much, it can well redouble." It is critical to take care of yourself in the aftermath of a suicide. I have heard from far too many survivors who share that they dealt with the suicide by not dealing with it at all. Instead they used drugs, alcohol, and sex to numb the pain, only to wake up ten or fifteen years later realizing their life is in shambles and they have not even scratched the surface in dealing with the suicide. When we avoid dealing with a major loss like this, it does not just go away. It grows and grows until we choose to look at it. You deserve much more than that. You deserve self-care and love.

I, both professionally and personally, strongly encourage you to make time for yourself, surround yourself with people whom you love and enjoy, and do what you need in order to walk through this journey in a healthy manner. You are worth it! Even when you do not believe it, trust me, you are worth it! If you do not take care of yourself, nobody else will either.

Questions to Consider

What are your thoughts on self-care?

Does self-care feel more necessary or selfish to you?

What types of things could you do to begin implementing self-care?

Are there any hobbies or areas of interest you could pursue during this time?

Are there any friends or family members you would like to see regularly and could schedule some time with on a consistent basis?

Sometimes practicing self-care involves limiting time with people who are not healthy for you. Do you have any people in your life that would be better for you to see less often?

CHAPTER 12

What about God?

WHEN I FIRST set out to write this book, I surveyed hundreds of survivors to ask them what type of content they felt should be in this resource. I expected the answers to ask for content on grief, trauma, and guilt. Surprisingly, the overwhelming response was to talk about God. The surveys indicated people wanted to know why God allowed their loved ones to die, why he didn't intervene, and if their loved ones were in Hell because they 'committed the unforgiveable sin.' I recognize not all readers believe in God, and many more are probably angry toward a God who would allow such a devastating act to take place, but with the number of responses pleading for this topic to be touched on, I think it's worth discussing.

We cannot know all of the answers to our questions, but a good place to start is by looking at God, his character, and how he feels about us. In order to get a better understanding of God, we need to go directly to the source. In my experience as a Christian I have learned it does us no good to assume what he thinks or how he operates; instead, we need to see what the Bible says.

God loves us desperately. That may sound far-fetched to some or even worthless to others, but the reality is God's love is overwhelming even when we don't fully understand or accept it. Sometimes we imagine God to be sitting high up in Heaven, out of reach, and judging all we say and do. Nothing could be further from the truth. God is a loving and gracious God that intimately understands our deepest pain and sorrow. God is not a distant God, aloof to our grief. Instead, He mourns with us and cares deeply. Here are a few verses to describe his love and concern for us:

Psalm 34:18 "The LORD is close to the brokenhearted and saves those who are crushed in spirit."
Psalm 56:8 (NLT) "You keep track of all my sorrows. You have collected all my tears in your bottle. You have recorded each one in your book."
Psalm 103:13 (NLT) "The LORD is like a father to his children, tender and compassionate to those who fear him."

The Psalms are full of verses explaining God's love for us, the comfort he provides, the strength he gives, and the compassion he expresses toward us. He recognizes our pain, understands our sorrow, and can fully relate to our grief. He loves us something fierce.

I think the obvious question here for most folks is: "If God is so loving, why didn't he heal our loved ones?" The truth is: I don't know. His denial to heal them from their pain and torment on Earth, though, does not lessen his goodness; it merely displays the reality of our fallen world. The reality is no answer to the question "why?" will be sufficient, similar to how no answer will be sufficient as to why our loved ones chose to die. We cannot receive comfort with logic when our hearts have been shattered. Hearts need mending and healing, not answers and reasons. A few friends and I were recently discussing this very concept, and I walked away with something more powerful than the question of "why?" Perhaps we have been asking the wrong question all along. Perhaps we should have been asking "Who?" as in, "Who is going to heal this shattered heart?"

Indeed, this is the real question! When we can resist the desire to ask why God allowed or failed to prevent the suicide and focus on who God is instead, we, in essence, discover the 'why' is not so important after all because, as mentioned above, the heart doesn't respond to logic. Rather, our focus should be on uncovering the character of God, the One who brings comfort. The One who *is* comfort.

In a well-known passage from Matthew 5:3-4, known as the Sermon on the Mount, Jesus says, "Blessed are the poor in spirit, for theirs is the kingdom of heaven. Blessed are those who mourn, for they will be comforted." What does this 'comfort' look like? How can God bring comfort to us when we only feel deep despair and sadness after this great loss? I think it looks different to each of us.

My mom died when I was only ten years old, and I was incredibly traumatized after finding her dead body. The scene has been stamped on my brain, impossible to forget. Knowing what I know now as a therapist, I can look back and clearly see I had developed all the signs of PTSD. In addition to this though, I also developed Obsessive Compulsive Disorder. Each night, I would go around the house, ensuring each door was locked, and the windows as well. I would then make sure the garage door was shut, too. My brain told me if I did not, my family would die. (OCD forces you to believe something horrible will happen if you don't do something perfectly.) Then, after I had finished checking all the locks, I feared I had accidentally unlocked a door during my checking, and so I would then re-check the entire house and garage again. I knew it was excessive, but I was too afraid to deviate from my routine. After my dad and brother went to bed, I would check the whole house again, fearing they may have unlocked what I had secured.

My nights were consumed with this ritual. My days, though, were just as exhausting. I believed if my shoes were not lined up just right, I would also die. I would check my backpack dozens of times on the way to school, making sure my homework was in my folder. Once I could confirm it was, I would then fear it fell out while last checking, and I would be forced to check again and again and again. Every aspect of my life was wrought with fear. I never mentioned it to anyone because I knew they would attempt to talk me out of checking things hundreds of times a day. They wouldn't understand the compulsion. I knew I couldn't give it up though, or my family would all be dead. I was consumed with fear and dread on a daily basis. This lasted for six years. Day and night for six years.

At the age of 16, I went to a summer camp where the Gospel of Jesus was shared with me for the first time. Initially, I thought it was cheesy and a bit embarrassing, really. But something about the character of God and his goodness pulled me in. I committed my life to Christ that week and, about a month later, I noticed something life-changing. I woke up early one morning and went outside to grab the newspaper. I was the first one awake and when I went to open the door, I realized it was already un-locked. Shocked, I stood back for a moment and tried to replay in my mind my lock-checking from the night before. *'How did this happen?'* I thought. I realized I had not checked the locks last night. In fact, as I stood there thinking, I realized I had not checked the locks a single time since return-ing from camp. Without me even recognizing it, God had taken away my need to obsess over locking doors, lining up shoes, and checking my back-pack. He, in the most gracious and loving fashion, brought comfort and healing to the deepest and most fearful parts of my soul. "Who is going to heal this shattered heart?" For me, the answer is clear. The One who brings comfort.

James 4:8a says, "Come near to God and He will come near to you." I have found this to be an honest promise he has made to us. When I sought him at summer camp, he met me in a very real and practical way. He began the healing process for the wreckage suicide had caused. The healing was not all at once, nor is it complete even today, but he began to bring comfort bit by bit as only a tender-hearted Savior can do.

His Plan

God did not 'plan' for my mom to die by suicide, nor do I think he planned for your loved one to die by suicide either. I think our loved ones chose suicide to relieve the pain they were experiencing and, in spite of that, God plans to 'give us hope and a future.' In the Bible, a young boy named Joseph was sold into slavery by his older brothers because they were jealous of him. Many, many years later, Pharaoh put Joseph in charge of all of Egypt in order to save the people from a great famine. During this time, he came into contact again with his brothers for the first time since they sold him into slavery, and he responded to them in this way:

Genesis 50:20 "You intended to harm me, but God intended it for good to accomplish what is now being done, the saving of many lives."

Our lives were dramatically turned upside down the day our loved ones ended their life. Sometimes the pain is so overwhelming, it feels like they ended ours as well. We would all choose to have never experienced this pain; however, I can see today, twenty-five years later, much good has come to my life in spite of the pain. Through the website I run, *The Gift of Second*, I have had strangers write me letters to say they were sincerely contemplating suicide but after seeing the effects my mom's suicide had on me, they cannot imagine putting their own child through the same torment and have sought help instead of ending their life. Just like the verse above reads, "...but God intended it for good to accomplish what is now being done, the saving of many lives." Are people's lives being saved because I am doing amazing work and deserve the credit? Absolutely not. People's lives are being saved because God is taking a horrible experience and giving us hope and a future. Again, "Who is going to heal this shattered heart?" Only God can.

One truth I think is so important for us to grab hold of is that God desperately loved the one who chose suicide. He did not want them to kill themselves. God was just as heartbroken as you and I were when they ended their life. He could have healed them, but because He chose not to does not indicate He did not love them or care for them.

When the wife of author C.S. Lewis passed away, he struggled to make meaning of his life and questioned how God could allow such a painful loss to occur. He wrote this in his journal:

When I lay these questions before God I get no answer. But a rather special sort of 'no answer.' It is not the locked door. It is more like a silent, certainly not uncompassionate, gaze. As though He shook His head not in refusal but waiving the question. Like, 'Peace, child; you don't understand.'

Is My Loved One in Hell Because They Died by Suicide?

Many survivors have explained they have had others tell them their loved one is now in Hell because they chose suicide. Nothing, I am sure, could be more painful than to hear this from others. So, what's the answer? Are our loved ones in Hell because they chose suicide? The answer to that question is, without a doubt, no, they are not.

Let's break this down a little bit. Is suicide a sin? Yes, it is. We are all sinners. Romans 3:23 explains, "For all have sinned and fall short of the glory of God." Suicide is a sin because it is the murder of a human even if it is against one's own self. God is clear on his stance in Exodus 20:13, "You shall not murder." Beyond the simple fact it is murder, God sees sin as anything that puts a wedge between Him and us. When we choose things or people over God, we sin. When we choose to take control of our lives instead of entrusting God with it, we sin. Choosing to end a life, even if it is our own, is not what God intended for us. Is suicide an inexcusable sin? Absolutely not!

No one sin is worse than the next. Murder, adultery, stealing, idolatry, suicide, gossip, slander, gluttony, rape, drunkenness—all are sins. None is worse than the next. Society makes a hierarchy of sin but God does not. Each sin has already been covered by Jesus on the cross, and none is too great for the One who made the ultimate sacrifice on our behalf. So, to answer the question: "Are our loved ones in Hell because of their suicide?" No, they are not.

Concluding Thoughts

I think, at the end of the day, we do not understand suicide. We feel life is unpredictable and chaotic and even scary. It's natural to want to place blame on anything or anyone we feel did not prevent this horrific loss or might have even caused it. To know the answers or even have a scapegoat can sometimes give us a sense of control when everything feels so out-of-control. It's okay to be mad at God for not preventing the suicide. It's okay to be angry at him. I think talking to God about it, whether it be in the form of yelling or writing it down, is cathartic. I think God wants to hear from us and even more, he wants to meet us where we are. Angry, tearful, heartbroken, confused, whatever our feelings, he can handle it and wants the opportunity to comfort us if we will allow it.

There is a song titled "Runaway," by Jess Ray, I appreciate. It is a description of God's undying love for us even when we are mad and reject him. I think Chorus 3 applies perfectly.

RUNAWAY
© JESS RAY MUSIC 2015

VERSE 1
I can see it in your eyes, that you're gonna run, you're gonna run
I can hear it in the way that you speak to me that you're gonna leave
And as you slip away, I will say
As you pack your things, I will sing

CHORUS 1
Even if you run away from me, over the mountains through the valleys,
I will not rest, but search east and west to bring you back with me
Even if you sail away from me across the oceans and the seas,
I will move again like the mighty wind and blow you back to me
I'm gonna move again like the mighty wind and blow you back to me

VERSE 2
I have seen this all before, It is all too familiar
But you will never see the bottom of my storehouses of love
So as you use the night to make your flight,
No choice that you will make or path you take will change my mind

CHORUS 2
Even if one day you decide, you will find somewhere else to hide
I will walk your way and call your name and wait for your reply.

Even if you make up in your mind, you don't want be by my side,
I will leave behind 99 oh that you'd be mine
I'm gonna leave behind 99 oh that you'd be mine

CHORUS 3
Even if you stomp and scream and huff, tell me that I'm not good
enough
I'll take every swing and every blow, until you know my love
Even if you beat upon my chest, tell me that you don't understand,
I will love you and teach you to love me again,
I'm gonna love you and teach you to love me again
I assume that with your connections you have permission for this?

Questions to Consider
Have you been angry at or confused with God for not intervening and
healing your loved one?
How does this make you view God?
Do you view God as loving and caring or distant and judgmental?
Do you think he really wants to hear from us? Do you think talking to
him about our feelings will actually make a difference for us?
Do you think he can heal your shattered heart?
Have you been told by others, or believe yourself, that your loved one is in
Hell for 'committing the unforgiveable sin'? How does it make you feel to
know he or she is not?

CHAPTER 13

Wisdom from Other Survivors

SOMETIMES THE ONLY thing helpful to a survivor is to hear from others who have experienced the same pain and devastation and, yet, survived themselves. I asked hundreds of fellow survivors what wisdom they would pass on to others and here are their answers. I hope they will speak truth, understanding, and hope to you in this overwhelming time.

"Just breathe. It's agony and confusion and pain and guilt and questioning running nonstop in your mind. It's normal to react that way. It's normal to cry, scream, push people away, reach for people, and fall apart. Day by day, you'll slowly come back up. Art, photography, hiking, whatever gives you solace—do it. Blast music, watch funny movies. Do what you can to just get through another day. And another. You'll always have days that knock you down, even months later. I'm at one year and I still fall back. I just do what I can to get through it. Reach out to other survivors, and try to remember the good times."

"It's not your fault."

"Do what's right for you, when it's right for you . . . not when others think is right for you. Everyone grieves differently and at different paces. Stay true to yourself. Try to think of positive and good times with your partner versus the bad and negative things. Make changes only if that's what you want to do. It has to be up to you to find comfort, solace, and peace and learn to live again. It will be different but you can still live life. I feel that's what our partners would want for us. The big thing also is to understand that other people (for the most part) have no clue what it's like to lose a spouse (unless they have, too). Most people mean well, and sometimes we have to understand that."

"There's no right or wrong way to grieve as long as it's not doing harm. There's also no time limit for grief. Everyone is different."

"Everything you are feeling is normal. Feel the grief. Don't run away from it through work, drugs, alcohol, or any other way."

"Give yourself permission to cry, and don't try to 'hold it off until later.' For me, the more I tried to fight or delay the tears the longer they would last once I did finally let loose. If I let them out when the wave first hits, then I'm 'done with it' and can move on with the rest of my day."

"I don't think any words make a difference. It's the hugs and just having someone around you that is helpful."

"The pain does not stay as intense in the following months and years."

"Don't beat yourself up with the 'what ifs' and 'I should haves.' It doesn't matter—what's done is done. Find peace that they are not suffering with mental illness anymore."

"Just try to hold on and breathe. Seek help from a therapist. Try to find peace, cry, and break down whenever you must."

"The worst part and yet the best part is that life goes on. God has a plan."

"They say time heals all pain...this is not true...you always feel the pain. You just learn to live day to day with it a little bit better than the day before. Nobody has answers, nobody knows why...many people hold on to those two things the most. Thinking about the best of memories is the most painful for me because I always question how someone who seemed so happy could ever really be living with such misery and I not even know it...but again...we have no answers. Survivors are the worst at beating themselves up over something we could never have controlled to begin with. We have support to move forward and away from hurting ourselves pondering the whys and what ifs. Utilize the resources. Learn to speak about it, whether you realize it or not, we all have one thing in common: we are still here. We have each other."

"Just know that this is a long process. One day you may feel pretty good and the next day you may be slammed with sadness, grief, pain, and all of the negative emotions you can imagine. Just understand this is normal and will be your new life. For how long I can't tell you because I have been here a year and still go through this. Hold on and hang in there; this has to get better."

"Everyone grieves in their own way. Do not, for any reason, blame yourself. I carried a lot of anger toward my mom for ending her life, until a very wise man shared this advice with me: 'Would you be mad at someone for dying of a heart attack? No, because their heart was sick and it was beyond their control. With suicide, the person's mind is sick, which is also beyond their control.' It was in that moment that all my anger toward my mom melted away. That changed my life forever, and if it can help one more person, then I'm happy. Also, allow yourself to grieve. Give yourself time to deal with the devastating blow you've received. And take your time. Suicide, in my opinion, is very different from any other type of death. There are many emotions and a lot of pain that comes along with losing a dear loved one to their own hand. Don't feel guilty for how you feel. And know, above all, that you're not alone. There are many people who are dealing with some of the same emotions. Reach out and allow people to help you. To any other survivors, my heart goes out to you. May God comfort you and give you the strength to survive your loss. God bless you each and every one."

"You are not alone."

"Try not to figure out the 'why?' It never will make sense and we will never know the real answers. Just breathe and cry; let the gut wrenching pain out or it will destroy you. Each day will bring different emotions, which are all scary but normal. I'm on my twelfth year without my son and it's still hard. I talk about my son; I post things on social media all the time about him and suicide. I hate that word but it's just a word—it doesn't define who my son was. He was my world and I will forever speak of him. I am proud of my son always."

"Be kind to yourself."

"I know it's hard to talk about but talk to people. I actually got more out of talking to friends than I did a counselor. Support groups are great too!"

"It has been thirty years for me since my mom took her life when I was 11. Every day brings with it new emotions and new questions. Try to remember the person as they were in happy times."

"Breathe and take one day at a time. That is enough for you in the beginning. That's all I was able to do. Let your feelings come, and go with them. Cry, scream, sleep, and I promise you it will get better with time. You learn how to cope and ride the waves of pain. My son took his own life almost 5 years ago. I am so sorry for your loss."

"Reach out, go out if you're alone and walk around where there are people—I guarantee someone will offer you a smile, you'll hear a baby giggle, see some beautiful flowers or a sunset and will realize that life can be good for us all. Rest, eat well, read, listen to your favorite music, and try to realize that you are worth it. You can work through a hard time and at the end of the night comes the dawn."

"Be kind to yourself. Others mean well but say dismissive cliché phrases that sting to your core. Do whatever it takes without harm to get you through the day. Everything you feel has already been felt- you are not alone even though this may be the loneliest path in life."

"Reach out to help others."

"Talk often about your loved one, say their name when talking about them. Share about them—happy times and sad times. Have open and honest conversations with your family and friends. Holding in your thoughts and feelings does not help. Laugh, cry, praise, scream. It all helps."

"It is ok to be sad and miss that person, but is not ok to be miserable and allow that death to rob you of your own joy and happiness. Still struggling with this twelve years later. Suicide grief is a complicated work in progress."

"It's not your fault. It's never your fault."

"There is a light at the end of the tunnel and it is not a train. Healing takes time, sometimes a lifetime. Do not compare yourself to others. You will smile and laugh again."

"Healing takes time and others might not understand, especially if they have not experienced a death by suicide, which leaves a lot of "what if" questions. Our loved ones were not thinking of others but only ending their pain of living. They don't realize what it can do to the survivors. Don't allow anyone to tell you how long to grieve or that you should be over it by now. It's your grieving time, not theirs. Find a group of survivors of suicide in person and/or online."

"Never feel ashamed of how you lost your loved one; learn from this horrific experience and help raise awareness. I'm fifteen months out from losing my dad, and my other siblings hide what the truth is. Just embrace the reality of what caused the death. Yes, I know it's horrible, but remember it was depression/other mental illness just as real as cancer that took your love one. Don't feel ashamed ever."

"Don't forget to breathe. Sometimes it is the only thing you have control of. Take as long as you need to grieve; it will come in waves. No one's experience is going to be exactly like yours. Be around others who will let you feel what you feel."

"I think it is important to try to remember people will hurt you during this time. If they haven't gone through it, they do not know what we have endured. We can't expect them to, really. They might say all the wrong things and do all the wrong things. Your story is going to be different than mine, and you might not know how to help me, and your story is different than mine and I might not know how to help you. In other words, don't let others offend you!"

"Just breathe. One day at a time. Be kind to yourself."

"You have nothing to be ashamed of. If you are Christian, you must know that God understands this."

"Take your time. Your grief is yours, uniquely yours. There is no time frame, but it does somehow get tolerable, yet it never goes away. Don't apologize for anything—be you and do you. Keep the faith and pray! It's a club none of us asked to join, but good members are in it."

"Write a letter to the one who has died. Write a letter to them every day or night. Keep them in a book. It was the single most useful thing that I did. Later I wrote a book about my experience and I drew on the letters that I had written. It took me about sixteen years to do this, so don't worry when others tell you, 'you have to move on.' Your grief has its own timeline and is not a measure of how much you loved the one who has died. After I wrote my book, my health improved, and I gained valuable distance on my grief. There is never a day that I do not remember my brother, but now I remember the good times and the love that we shared. I pray that this will be your future too."

"They genuinely believed that you would be better off without them. They were ill."

"It's not your fault, you are not alone, and healing takes time."

"BREATHE."

"I understand exactly how you feel. This is going to be a very difficult journey, but you can find life and happiness again."

"You are not alone; there are those that truly understand. Tell us all about it and then tell us again."

"What you are experiencing is normal. Feeling like you are losing your mind and the inability to focus or concentrate are all expected. Give yourself grace to get through them. Be honest with yourself and those around you about what you need."

"Get prompt access to another (seasoned) suicide loss survivor."

"It wasn't your fault. Feel the feelings. Cry, cry, cry."

"No two people grieve the same way. Your relationship with that person was your own, and therefore, your grieving might be different than others."

"You are not alone. You will have good and bad days. Don't beat yourself up. Different people grieve in different ways for the same person. Although you will never get over your loss, your grief won't always be so overwhelming, and it is possible to feel happy again."

"I understand and I feel your devastation."

"You are not alone. Reach out to others. Share your story. Let yourself grieve, and don't feel guilty about it."

"If you feel it, acknowledge it, and don't let anyone tell you shouldn't feel that way. Listen to your own emotions and physical reactions. Talk. And if something is important for you to do while grieving, don't let anyone tell you it's wrong."

Questions to Consider

Which word of wisdom resonated the most with you?

How does it feel to know other people have experienced the same pain and devastation?

What kind of wisdom would you pass on to someone else at this point?

CHAPTER 14

Resources

THIS CHAPTER IS one of the most important in this book. It is imperative to know you are not alone. Millions of fellow survivors have experienced this horrible grief and, as a result, have made countless resources available. Specifically, survivors will find a wealth of online communities and groups on which to lean while navigating life after a suicide.

I have included organizations, websites, support groups, and books in this chapter. This list is not exhaustive by any means, but it is a great starting point for connecting with others. This list was compiled after asking hundreds of survivors what has been helpful to them. If one is not a good match for you, I urge to keep looking until you find one that is.

Some of the books below do contain triggering details pertaining to the exact nature of a suicide, and I want to encourage you to use discretion when reading any of these resources. If it becomes too overwhelming, stop reading, as nothing beneficial comes from traumatizing yourself.

Online and Community Support

American Foundation for Suicide Prevention (AFSP): (afsp.org) Contains resources for survivors as well as a search option for in-person support groups in your area.

American Association of Suicidology (AAS): (suicidology.org) Offers online support as well as an annual national conference for survivors.

Tragedy Assistance Program for Survivors (TAPS): (taps.org/suicide) This is a wonderful resource for survivors of military related suicides and a fabulous organization overall.

The Gift of Second: (thegiftofsecond.com) Offers hope, encouragement, and connection through blogs and videos for anyone impacted by a loved one's suicide. No traumatic/triggering details are allowed on this site.

Our Side of Suicide: (oursideofsuicide.com) Offers blogs written by survivors for survivors.

Survivors of Suicide Loss: (soslsd.org) Offers online support with educational newsletters as well in-person support groups and events for those impacted by suicide.

Suicide Awareness Voices of Education (SAVE): (save.org) Offers wonderful resources and educational information pertaining to grief.

Survivors of Suicide Bereavement Support Association (SOSBSA): (sosbsa.org.au) Offers bereavement assistance and support groups to those in Australia.

Kidsaid: (kidsaid.com) Is 'a safe place for kids to help each other deal with grief and loss.'

Suicide: Finding Hope: (suicidefindinghope.com) Available to help people as 'they navigate this journey.'

Friends in Grief: (friendsingrief.ca) A Canadian organization offering a variety of services to bereaved individuals.

Alliance of Hope: (allianceofhope.org) Offers an online communication forum with thousands of survivors where members can connect.

Also, there are several support groups on Facebook. Most are closed groups that simply require you asking to join, which will then give you access to thousands of other survivors. Search the following group names to find them: Survivors of Suicide, SOS-Survivors of Suicide, Survivors of Suicide Bereavement Support, SOS Fast, SOLOS.

Support Groups

The Dougy Center: (dougy.org) "Provides support in a safe place where children, teens, young adults, and their families grieving a death can share their experiences."

Friends for Survival: (friendsforsurvival.org) Offers in-person support groups in California and a national monthly newsletter containing helpful insight from fellow survivors.

Heartbeat Grief Support: (heartbeatsurvivorsaftersuicide.org) One of the national pioneers of in-person support groups with meetings taking place all over the country.

Survivors of Loved Ones to Suicide (SOLOS): (solossurvivorsoflovedonestosuicide.com) Offers both online and in-person support groups for survivors both nationally and internationally.

Compassionate Friends: (compassionatefriends.org) Offers support and groups to those who have lost a child. This is not a suicide-specific resource but several people mentioned this resource as helpful after their loved one's suicide.

American Foundation for Suicide Prevention (AFSP): (afsp.org) Search this website to find support groups in your city. This database contains groups found in the United States, Australia, Brazil, Canada, and China.

Canadian Association for Suicide Prevention (CASP): (suicideprevention.ca) In addition to assisting the public with suicide prevention resources, CASP also offers groups and resources for survivors of suicide loss.

Events

International Survivors of Suicide Loss Day: (afsp.org) This day typically takes place the Saturday before Thanksgiving and has groups from all over the world meet in hundreds of cities worldwide. The event includes support from other survivors, speakers, resources, as well as the opportunity to screen a newly released documentary for survivors.

Camp Kita: (campkita.com) is a free week-long summer camp program open to children ages 8-17 who are survivors of a loved one's suicide.

Out of the Darkness Walks: (afsp.org) Walks connect survivors with one another while also fundraising to both help prevent suicide and provide resources for those impacted by it.

Books

Finding Peace without All the Pieces After a Love One's Suicide by LaRita Archibald

The Best Little Girl Says Goodbye: A Therapist Grieves by Blanche Goodwin.

Do They Have Good Days in Heaven? by Michelle Linn-Gust

Why People Die by Suicide by Thomas Joiner

Grieving a Suicide by Albert Hsu

My Son, My Son by Iris Bolton

Prayers for Bobby by Leroy Aarons

A Mother's Reckoning by Sue Klebold

Sibling Suicide: Journey from Despair to Hope by Nate Wagner

No Time to Say Goodbye by Carla Fine

Rocky Roads by Michelle Linn-Gust

Understanding Your Suicide Grief by Alan Wolfelt

Grief After Suicide by Jack Jordon & John McIntosh

Alive in Heaven by Mark Canfora

Healing After Loss: Daily Meditations for Working through Grief by Martha Whitmore Hickman.

The Dougy Center has several books, DVDs, and brochures for children and teens available. Some suicide-specific resources are available as well, but most focus on death and loss in general (dougy.org).

Acknowledgements

MANY PEOPLE HAVE showed an incredible amount of love, support, and encouragement while I created this project. Without them, this book would never have made it past chapter one.

David: Thanks for the continued encouragement, shared vision, and the keys to quiet. I love everything about you—you really are the best!

Munchkins: You are all so sweet and adorable—how did I get so lucky? You make me want to be the mom I wish I had. I pray my actions never cause you to doubt my love or your worth.

Kelly: You are the one who started this entire adventure. You will always hold such a special place in my heart. I could sit with you at the airport all day!

Bethany: You deserve a special seat in Heaven for the amount of work, time, and creativeness you have donated to me and my projects. Thank you!

Kimberly: Whether you are making me a diagram (again) or making me laugh, I cannot thank you enough! #thebest

Stu: Thank you for your patience and wisdom as I wrestled. Bless you!

Acknowledgements

Jill and Deidre: Thank you, thank you, thank you! I have no words to describe my appreciation for you both. Thank you for making my words flow!

Janae, Karianne, and Megan: You three make my life so sweet and fun. I need laughter to survive, and you girls bring it! You are gifts to my soul.

Margy: What an unexpected gift I was given all those years ago when I met you! May you never doubt your impact on my life. Thanks for walking with me on this journey and your generosity in the process. (All spoken in a British accent, of course).

Robin: Thanks for the continual 'check-ins' on the book and life. I appreciate your truth, humor, and our shared greatest adventure ever!

FTL Writing: You girls bring the humor, wisdom, assistance, and encouragement like nothing I have experienced before now. What was life like before y'all? A true gift from above!

Notes

Introduction: A Letter from The Author

1. "Page Turner: This Week in Fiction: Mohsin Hamid," by Cressida Leyshon, newyorker.com, September 16, 2012, http:www.newyorker.com/books/page-turner/this-week-in-fiction-mohsin-hamid, accessed June 10, 2016.
2. The Gift of Second: thegiftofsecond.com.
3. Brené Brown, "Listening to Shame," TED, Long Beach, California, March 2012, http:www.ted.com/talks/brene_brown_listening_to_shame?language=en, accessed June 10, 2016.

Chapter1: The Path of Grief

1. Earl A. Grollman, Straight Talk about Death for Teenagers, (Boston: Beacon Press, 1993), 6.
2. C.S. Lewis, *A Grief Observed* (New York: Harper One, 1961), XII.
3. Tony Dungy, *Quiet Strength: A Memoir*, (Carol Stream: Tyndale House Publishers, INC, 2007), 263.
4. "Complicated Grief," mayoclinic.com, last modified September 13, 2014, http://www.mayoclinic.org/diseases-conditions/complicated-grief/basics/symptoms/con-20032765, accessed June 10, 2016.
5. Katherine Shear, Sidney Zisook, "Grief and Bereavement: What Psychiatrists Need to Know," *World Psychiatry*, 8(2) (June 2009): 67-74. www.ncbi.nlm.nih.gov/pmc/articles/PMC2691160, accessed June 10, 2016.

6. Anne Lamott, *Traveling Mercies: Some Thoughts on Faith*, (New York: Pantheon Books, 1999), 68.

Chapter 2: Guilt and Shame

1. Elisabeth Kübler-Ross, *On Death and Dying*, (New York: Macmillan Publishing Co., 1969), 161.
2. Merriam-Webster's Collegiate Dictionary, 11ᵗʰ ed., s.v. "guilt".
3. LaRita Archibald, *Reinforcement in the Aftermath of Suicide*, 1985.
4. Albert C. Cain, ed., *Survivors of Suicide*, (Springfield: Charles C. Thomas, 1972), X.

Chapter 3: Trauma and PTSD

1. Laurell K. Hamilton, Mistral's Kiss, (New York: Random House, 2010), PDF e-book.
2. Margy Grebe, Conversation with author, March 2016.

Chapter 4: Therapy and Groups

1. Kay Redfield Jamison, *Night Falls Fast: Understanding Suicide* (New York: Alfred A. Knopf, 1999), 295.
2. To find out more about EMDR or to find a clinician in your area trained in this technique, check out their website at www.emdr.com.
3. Marilyn Koenig, conversation with author, November, 2015.
4. Heather Thompson, "12 Life Lessons from Mister Rogers," parade.com, last modified February 27, 2015, http://parade.com/379451/hthompson/12-life-lessons-from-mister-rogers/.

Chapter 5: Communicating About Suicide

1. Stan Margulies and David L. Wolper. "Willy Wonka & The Chocolate Factory", directed by Mel Stuart, (Burbank, CA: Warner Home Video, 2001), DVD.

2. Carla Fine, No Time to Say Goodbye, (New York: Broadway Books, 1997), 68.

Chapter 6: What Helped Other Survivors

1. Eva Ibbotson, The Dragonfly Pool, (New York: Puffin Books, 2008), PDF e-book.
2. Elizabeth Gilbert, Eat Pray Love, (New York: Penguin Group, 2006), 71.
3. Iris Murdoch, *The Sacred and Profane Love Machine*, (Penguin Books, 1974) 30,31.
4. Ann Roiphe, *Epilogue: A Memoir*, (New York: Harper Perennial, 2008), 4.
5. "Gail Sheehy on America's Passage," belief.net, last modified 2003, http://beliefnet.com/ inspiration/2003/09/gail-sheehy-on-americas-passage.aspx?, last accessed july 4, 2016.
6. American Foundation for Suicide Prevention (afsp.org) has several resources to help survivors.

Chapter 7: Incomprehensible Death

1. Alison Wertheimer, *A Special Scar: The Experienced of People Bereaved by Suicide*, (Philadelphia, Taylor & Francis, 2004), PDF e-book.
2. Richard Russo, ed., *A Healing Touch: True Stories of Life, Death, and Hospice* (Camden: Down East Books, 2008), 107-108.
3. Kay Redfield Jamison, *Night Falls Fast: Understanding Suicide*, 73.
4. Ibid., 85.
5. LaRita Archibald, *Reinforcement in the Aftermath of Suicide*, 1985.

Chapter 8: Forgiveness

1. Marianne Williamson, *Illuminata: Thoughts, Prayers, Rites of Passage*, (New York: Riverhead Books, 1995), 131-132.

2. R.T. Kendall, *Total Forgiveness*, (Lake Mary: Charisma House, 2002), 23-31.
3. Ibid., 30.
4. Merriam-Webster's Collegiate Dictionary, 11th ed., s.v. "forgive".
5. Darnell Young,"But So Am I," *The Gift of Second*, last modified May 15, 2016, http://thegiftofsecond.com/2016/05/but-so-am-i-by-darnell-young/.
6. R.T. Kendall, *Total Forgiveness*, 159.
7. Ibid., 149.

Chapter 9: How A Specific Loss Effects How We Grieve

1. Lisa Goich, *14 Days: A Mother, A Daughter, A Two-Week Goodbye*, (Savio Republic, 2015), PDF e-book.
2. All survivor quotes gathered from interviews, surveys, or discussions with the author.
3. Carl Jung, *Modern Man in Search of a Soul*, (New York: Routledge, 2001), 62.

Chapter 10: The First Year

1. Nicholas Sparks, *Message in a Bottle*, (New York: Grand Central Publishing, 1998), PDF e-book.
2. Tessa Shaffer, *Heaven Has No Regrets*, (Harrisburg: Create Space, 2014), 73.
3. John Irving, A Prayer for Owen Meany, (New York: William Morrow, 1989), 128.

Chapter 11: Self-Care

1. Audre Lorde, A Burst of Light: Essays, (Ithica, Firebrand Books, 1988), 131.
2. Bill Jenkins, *What to Do When the Police Leave: A Guide to the First Days of Traumatic Loss*, (Richmond: WBJ Press, 2001), 5.

Chapter 12: What about God?

1. Lewis, *A Grief Observed*, 69.
2. Jess Ray, "Runaway," Sentimental Creatures, Jess Ray Music, 2016, compact disc.

Chapter 13: Wisdom from Other Survivors

1. All quotes gathered from survivors in the form of interviews, anonymous surveys, discussions, and questionnaires.

About the Author

BRANDY LIDBECK IS a licensed marriage and family therapist who lives in California with her husband and kiddos. She enjoys sports, naps, the mountains, and loves speaking truth to those vulnerable places in our hearts. Brandy is also the creator of *The Gift of Second*, a website for those impacted by a loved one's suicide (thegiftofsecond.com).

41401541R00073

Made in the USA
San Bernardino, CA
11 November 2016